MEDIA, FEMINISM, CULTURAL STUDIES

The Cinema of Hayao Miyazaki
by Jeremy Mark Robinson

The Poetry of Cinema
by John Madden

I0185651

The Sacred Cinema of Andrei Tarkovsky
by Jeremy Mark Robinson

Jean-Luc Godard: The Passion of Cinema / Le Passion de Cinéma
by Jeremy Mark Robinson

Liv Tyler: Star In Ascendance
by Thomas A. Christie

The Cinema of Richard Linklater
by Thomas A. Christie

Walerian Borowczyk
by Jeremy Mark Robinson

Stepping Forward: Essays, Lectures and Interviews
by Wolfgang Iser

Wild Zones: Pornography, Art and Feminism
by Kelly Ives

Global Media Warning: Explorations of Radio, Television and the Press
by Oliver Whitehorne

'Cosmo Woman': The World of Women's Magazines
by Oliver Whitehorne

Andrea Dworkin
by Jeremy Mark Robinson

Cixous, Irigaray, Kristeva: The Jouissance of French Feminism
by Kelly Ives

FORTHCOMING BOOKS

BLADE RUNNER

POCKET MOVIE GUIDE

Blade Runner

Pocket Movie Guide

JEREMY MARK ROBINSON

Crescent Moon

First published 2013.
© Jeremy Mark Robinson 2013.

Printed and bound in the U.S.A.
Set in Rotis SemiSans, 9 on 14pt.
Designed by Radiance Graphics.

British Library Cataloguing in Publication data available for this title.

ISBN-13 9781861714466 (Pbk)

Crescent Moon Publishing
P.O. Box 1312
Maidstone, Kent
ME14 5XU, Great Britain
www.crmoon.com

CONTENTS

ACKNOWLEDGEMENTS

To the authors and publishers quoted.
To the copyright holders of the illustrations.
To Warner Brothers. The Blade Runner Partnership.

Other images courtesy of Universal; 20th Century Fox; Carolco; Warner Brothers; Warner Independent; Lion's Gate; DreamWorks; Paramount; Moebius; MGM; Miramax; Lucasfilm; Sony/ Columbia; and Columbia/ TriStar.

Many thanks to Sheena Duggal, Irene Rodríguez and Thomas Christie.

ABBREVIATIONS

FN   *Future Noir* by Paul Sammon

(© The Blade Runner Partnership/ Warner Bros.)

1

THE CINEMA OF PHILIP K. DICK

The greatest menace in the 20th century is the totalitarian state. It can take many forms: left-wing fascism, psychological movements, religious movements, drug rehabilitation places, powerful people, manipulative people; or it can be in a relationship with someone who is more powerful than you psychologically. Essentially, I'm pleading the case of those people who are not strong. If I were strong myself I would probably not feel this as such a menace.

Philip K. Dick[1]

Philip Kindred Dick (1928-1982) was a key figure in 20th century science fiction, famous for embracing drugs and the counter-culture in his work. Dick's themes included perception and reality, drug-taking, state control, global capitalism, surveillance, and paranoia.[2] Dick's fiction includes *The Man In the High Castle, Flow My Tears, The Policeman Said, A Scanner Darkly, The Game Players of Titan, Clan of the Alphane Moon, The Three Stigmata of Palmer Eldritch, Do Androids Dream of Electric Sheep?, Valis, The Divine Invasion, Martian Time-Slip, The Minority Report*, and *We Can Remember It For You Wholesale*.

Born on December 16, 1928 in Chicago, Philip Kindred

---

1 Quoted in C. Platt, 150.
2 For John Baxter, Phil Dick was 'the one sf author that people outside of the sf readership tend to know about, in the same way that Tolkien is the one fantasy author that people have heard of. In the case of Dick I think he's not regarded as a sf writer by many people because he never wrote hard, technological sf, it was more sociological, state-of-consciousness sort of stuff. He had a cult following that extended beyond the purely sf crowd' (in J. Brosnan, 1991, 384).

Dick lived most of his life in California. He studied at Berkeley High School, and for a short period in 1949 at the University of California. He was married five times, and had three children (Laura Archer, Isa Dick Hackett and Christopher Kenneth). He died on March 2, 1982 in Santa Ana. Dick mainly worked in the science fiction zone. He wrote 121 short stories and 44 novels.

Movies based on Philip K. Dick's fiction include: *Blade Runner* (1982), *Total Recall* (1990),[3] *Minority Report* (2002),[4] *A Scanner Darkly* (2006),[5] *Confessions d'un Barjo* (1992, a French movie based on 1959's *Confessions of a Crap Artist*), a Canadian film, *Screamers* (1995),[6] based on Dick's *Second Variety* story, *Paycheck*, directed by John Woo,[7] *Next* (Lee

---

3 *Total Recall* was based on Philip K. Dick's story "We Can Remember It For You Wholesale" (1966) about a man, Douglas Quail (it's Quaid in the film), who undergoes a memory implant operation as a luxury vacation trip to Mars; the Rekal people find out he was an Interplan agent whose real memory had been buried under artificial memories; several plot twists later, it is not certain which Quaid is the 'real' one, which story is the true one, and so on.

4 *Minority Report* starred Tom Cruise as John Anderton, a cop who works for the 'Pre-Crime' division in a futuristic Washington, in 2054. Anderton is part of a team that prevents crimes (in particular, murders) before they've been committed, with the aid of three 'pre-cogs', humanoid mutants. Scott Frank, Jon Cohen, Frank Darabont, John August, and others, wrote the script for *Minority Report* from Philip K. Dick's 1956 short story (which appeared in *Fantastic Universe* in January, 1956). Rated 'PG-13' and released in the U.S.A. in mid-June, 2002, *Minority Report* ran for 144 minutes. It grossed $342m around the world.

5 *A Scanner Darkly* (1977) was directed by Richard Linklater in 2006.
6 The Canadian *Screamers* (Christian Duguay, 1995) starred Peter Weller as the chief of a mining colony on a remote planet (Sirius 6B) quarrying a radioactive superfuel (berynium) in the year 2078. It was based on a Philip K. Dick story ("Second Variety", 1953), with a script co-written by Dan O'Bannon and Miguel Tejada-Flores. Franco Battista and Tom Berry produced for Triumph Films/ Sony. *Screamers* was essentially a sci-fi thriller/ chase movie with some *Alien* horror added.

7 *Paycheck* (Paramount/ DreamWorks, 2003) was a Philip K. Dick story made over as a John Woo action thriller. All of the usual elements of a John Woo actioner were there: the elaborate gun battles, car and motorbike chases, lots of explosions, plenty of slow motion, multiple cameras – hell, Woo even squeezed in his customary lyrical shots of flying birds (and Christian motifs). But *Paycheck* wasn't a patch on John Woo classics such as *Hard-Boiled* and *The Killer* (and Ben Affleck was no Chow Yun-Fat, either).

Tamahori, 2007),[8] based on *The Golden Man,* and *Impostor* (Gary Fleder, 2002).[9]

The more recent cycle of Philip Kindred Dick movies began with *Minority Report*[10] and *Impostor* in 2002 – *Paycheck* and *Next* followed in 2003 and 2007, and *The Owl In Daylight,* a movie about Dick (rumoured in 2009), and *Radio Free Alemuth* (2010). A sequel to *Screamers*[11] (*Screamers 2: The Bloodening* – no, sorry, it was subtitled *The Hunting*) was released in 2009 (again shooting in Canada).[12] In 2011, *The Adjustment Bureau*[13] (dir. George

8 *Next* (Paramount, dir. Lee Tamahori, 2007) was a star vehicle for Nic Cage (although Julianne Moore shared the name above the title credit). Jason Koornick, Todd Gamer, Norm Golightly, Ben Waisbren, Gary Goldman, Graham King, Arne Schmidt and Cage produced. It was co-scripted by Jonathan Hensleigh, Paul Bernbaum and Gary Goldman, who had co-written *Total Recall.* Nic Cage played Cris, a minor Las Vegas magician who has the ability to see into the future – only two minutes into the future, but for some reason (it's lerrrrv, folks!), he can see the love of his life, Liz (Jessica Biel) days or maybe years into the future.

9 *Impostor* (Dimension Films/ Miramax, directed by Gary Fleder, 2002) starred Gary Sinise, Madeleine Stowe and Vincent d'Onofrio in a feature film based on Philip K. Dick's 1953 short story of the same name. Scott Rosenberg, Caroline Case, Ehren Kruger and David Twohy scripted. Michael Phillips produced. Everything associated with sci-fi cinema and Dick adaptions was in full effect: man on the run story, a slick, hi-tech look, paranoia, urban decay, tons of action beats, stunts, visual fx, and 1000s of additions to Dick's text.

10 *Minority Report* is something like how *Blade Runner* would be if it were made today.

11 *Screamers* had a similar ending to *Blade Runner*: the hero and heroine, Jessica (Jennifer Rubin, who's been replaced by a robot) hope to escape in a small craft away from the chaos and their former lives. It's a guy falling for a robot, yet again (complete with goodbye kiss), and *Screamers'* ending consciously evokes *Blade Runner.*

12 The 2009 sequel *Screamers 2: The Hunting* delivered a dull story (a routine sci-fi scenario of answering a distress call from a planet, like an episode in any space opera TV series), in an unimaginative manner. Boring characters, corny situations, tedious action, cynical attitudes, zero humour, and with little-to-no Philip K. Dick content (*Screamers 2* was a sequel to the 1995 movie, not Dick's "Second Variety" tale, and the first movie had already departed far from the story).

Ultimately, *Screamers 2* was pointless. My kids have made way better movies using a video camera in the local woods. Borrowings from the *Alien* and *Terminator* movies (and plenty of other sci-fi and horror flicks) didn't help, and the low budget was used as an excuse for a lame, totally predictable script (Akira Kurosawa and Ingmar Bergman were able to deliver masterpieces on far lower budgets. But then, not everybody is a Kurosawa or a Bergman!).

13 The 2011 Universal production was the subject of duelling lawsuits: the case brought by Phil Dick's estate (run by two of his daughters) claimed that the rights to the story material had been sold to director George Nolfi for $75,000 back in 2001 (a bargain price!), on the understanding that revenue would be shared when the movie was produced and released (the film cost $62 million, and grossed $127 million). Universal and the production company Media Rights Capital meanwhile claimed that the story, published in 1954, was now in the public domain.

Nolfi) with Matt Damon and Emily Blunt appeared, a Dick story as a lerrrve story.[14] *King of the Elves* was in the works from the Walt Disney Company, an animated feature to be released in 2012.[15] A remake of *Total Recall* appeared in 2012.

PHILIP K. DICK AT THE GLOBAL BOX OFFICE

A striking aspect of the films made from the fiction of Philip K. Dick is how many are very high budget movies (*Paycheck, Minority Report, Blade Runner, Next* and *Total Recall*), and just how many high profile filmmakers have been attracted to Dick's stories: Ridley Scott, Paul Verhoeven, John Woo and the most successful film director of recent times, Steven Spielberg. Those four directors together have generated billions globally.

The high budget films produced from Philip K. Dick's stories come in at \$102 million (*Minority Report*), \$28 million (*Blade Runner*) and 60 million bucks for *Total Recall* (in contemplating budgets there are numerous factors to take into account – not least the period in which the film was produced: *Blade Runner* costing in the region of \$28 million was not unknown for a big budget movie made in 1981-82; by the end of the decade, budgets had escalated enormously).[16]

Filmmakers came to Philip K. Dick at different stages in their careers, too: by the time Steven Spielberg took up Dick's short story, he was a veteran of some of the most successful films in cinema history, and was particularly known for his science fiction and fantasy movies (*Jurassic*

14 Hey, whaddya know, *The Adjustment Bureau* featured yet another man/ couple on the run, pursed by a nefarious government organization. The most enjoyable aspect of *The Adjustment Bureau* was the location shooting in New York City. I never get tired of visiting Gotham and seeing it in movies.
15 Stage and radio productions have included an opera based on *VALIS*, and plays of *Do Androids Dream of Electric Sheep?* and *Flow My Tears, the Policeman Said*.
16 The average negative cost for a Hollywood movie rose from \$9.4 million in 1980 to \$26.8 million in 1990 (and \$39 million in 1995). The average cost for domestic P & A (prints and advertizing) rose from \$4.3 million in 1980 to \$11.6m in 1990 to \$20 million in 1995. *Blade Runner* took \$27m gross at the US box office.

Park, Close Encounters, E.T., Hook, etc).

John Woo was another veteran, who produced *Paycheck* with his regular producer Terence Chang after making the move to Hollywood from China, and turning in a series of big actioners: *Broken Arrow, Face-Off* and *Mission Impossible 2*. Paul Verhoeven was another veteran of many features, who moved to America for *RoboCop.* Ridley Scott was also a visitor: *Blade Runner* was his third film (after a successful career in TV commercials), and his third Hollywood movie (although his previous two films, *Alien* and *The Duellists*, had been shot in Europe). Richard Linklater, meanwhile, is one of the few independent filmmakers to take on Philip K. Dick (although Linklater became more mainstream and establishment over the years).

SCI-FI CINEMA AND PHILIP K. DICK'S CINEMA

> I was beginning to sense that what we perceived was not what was actually there. I was interested in Jung's idea of projection – what we experience as external to us may really be projected from out of the unconscious, which means of course that each person's world has to be somewhat different from everybody else's, because the contents of each person's unconscious will be to a certain extent unique.

> Philip K. Dick[17]

Blade Runner, Total Recall, Minority Report and other Philip K. Dick movies were part of a general trend in Hollywood cinema towards fantasy and the fantastic: after the success of *Star Wars*, space opera, sci-fi, and fantasy became staples in Hollywood A-list output: *E.T.* (1982), *The Black Hole* (1979), the *Superman* series (1978 onwards), the *Alien* series (1979 onwards), the *Star Trek* films (1979 onwards), the *Mad Max* series (1979 onwards), *Ghostbusters* (1984), *The Last Starfighter* (1984), *Gremlins* (1984), *RoboCop* (1987), *Total Recall* (1990), *Tron* (1982), *Brainstorm* (1983), *The Abyss* (1989), *Escape From New York* (1981), *The Thing*

17 Quoted in C. Platt, 149.

(1982), the *Terminator* films (1984 onwards), the *Back to the Future* films (1985 onwards), and the sword-and-sorcery fantasies: *The Beastmaster* (1983), *Ladyhawke* (1985), *Willow* (1988), *Krull* (1983), *Conan the Barbarian* (1982), *Dragonslayer* (1981), *The Dark Crystal* (1983), *The Sword and the Sorcerer* (1982), and *Labyrinth* (1987).

The successes of the pictures of the late 1970s and early 1980s, the highpoint of the Lucas-Spielberg era, with their heavy sci-fi and fantasy content, would lead towards the more recent Philip K. Dick adaptions, including *Minority Report, Screamers,* and *A Scanner Darkly.*

For John Baxter, sci-fi films became increasingly superficial and visual in the 1980s, with fewer ideas and science fiction in them. It was all about action and visuals, made by people with no feeling or understanding for sci-fi. *Blade Runner,* Baxter said, was 'ravishingly visual – a wonderful film to look at', but its ideas were 'really aboriginal'.[18]

❀

Blade Runner, Minority Report, Total Recall and other Philip K. Dick adaptions tend towards the 'intellectual', 'thoughtful' or 'philosophical' type of sci-fi movie (although both *Minority Report, Next, Impostor, Paycheck* and *Total Recall* are very much also firmly part of the action genre). One of the more intriguing of Dick's concerns was the role of spirituality and religion in contemporary society, and the links between the spiritual and alternate realities (such as drug states).

In some respects, science fiction and fantasy films have replaced the religious movies of the 1950s and 1960s. The move is embodied by the shift from the 1950s *The Ten Commandments* to the 1970s *Close Encounters of the Third Kind.* Cinema's space aliens are the new gods, the divine beings who live in the sky and come down from Heaven.

Blade Runner buys into that view in a number of ways, from its evocations of religious awe at the spectacle of the city of Los Angeles of the future, to its depiction of the replicants as rebel angels (to reinforce that allusion, Roy Batty quotes from British religious poets John Milton, Percy Bysshe Shelley and William Blake). In *Minority Report,*

18 Quoted in J. Brosnan, 1991, 382.

meanwhile, the pre-cogs are worshipped as modern-day saints, with a cult building up around them. The sequel to *Blade Runner,* had it appeared, would have explored the spiritual aspects of the replicants.

It's not remarkable that aliens, UFOs and science fiction and fantasy should comprise the new religious element in movies. In a secular, technological age, old-fashioned deities would no longer hold sway; instead, beings with enhanced technological capabilities would be worshipped. The new frontier in the contemporary world is not the American West, but outer space, as the space race demonstrated.[19] The sky, as Mircea Eliade said, is one of the origins of the sacred, of the feeling for the holy: the sky is the ultimate Other, infinite and awe-inspiring. Gods have since earliest times inhabited celestial realms.

♣

The typical Philip K. Dick film has some McGuffin or narrative hook that's used as the basis for the story: in *Paycheck* and *Minority Report* it's seeing into the future, in *Blade Runner* it's androids, in *A Scanner Darkly* it's drugs, and in *Total Recall* it's memory implants (also used in *Blade Runner).*

Philip K. Dick's fictions are often but not always set in America (North America, that is). Most of the Dick adaptions have been set in the U.S.A., with *Screamers* and *Total Recall* going to other planets.[20] (Maybe it's significant that four of the key Phil Dick films have been helmed by people who came to Hollywood already established in their home countries as filmmakers: Ridley Scott, Paul Verhoeven, Lee Tamahori and John Woo. Maybe Dick's fiction requires the viewpoint of a visitor or outsider to tease out the potential in the texts).

But only *A Scanner Darkly* and *Next* take place in a world very similar to present-day America (although *A Scanner Darkly* is meant to be a few years in the future): *Minority Report, Blade Runner, Impostor, Total Recall* and *Paycheck* are set in the future (*Minority Report* is fifty years

19 The frontier is now outer space, as sci-fi fiction and films have often explored: Mars in Dick's fiction, or the mining and industrial colonies and outposts in films such as *Starship Troopers, Serenity, Screamers* and *Alien.*
20 *Second Variety,* on which *Screamers* is based, was set on Earth.

hence; *Screamers* and *Impostor* are set in the late 2070s; *Paycheck* is a few years off; *Blade Runner* is 37 years after 1982, when the film was released, though 2019 ain't so far away now). Of course, all of Dick's stories, like all future sci-fi stories, are always about right now (or about when they were written).

The Phil Dick films are stuffed with hardware – with computers, cameras, screens, digital billboards, cool flying machines, cool cars, time machines, scanners, lie detectors, guns, and endless cities. Those cities may have their dark underbellies, but they are still amazing places to live.

Blade Runner was partly a picture about all-pervading technology (as with *2001: A Space Odyssey, Akira* and *Star Wars*). In *Blade Runner*, however, technology was viewed ambiguously and anxiously, as well as rapturously. While the filmmakers celebrated the sublime aspects of technology (the spinners flying over a sprawling metropolis, for example, or the video phones), the characters within the piece struggle with technology. *Blade Runner* is like many a science fiction picture in seeing advanced technology as highly problematic – the emphasis on surveillance, the invasion of privacy and the breakdown of identity, for instance, are recurring themes in sci-fi cinema.

Philip K. Dick adaptions tend to be conceived as star vehicles for male stars: Tom Cruise, Arnold Schwarzenegger, Nic Cage, Keanu Reeves and Harrison Ford. And because they are star vehicles for major stars, with the stars in most every scene, they become a particular kind of movie: big budget and big action.

Apart from *Blade Runner* and *A Scanner Darkly*, most Philip K. Dick movies tend to be conceived as action-adventure films, usually within a thriller narrative. So the chases are longer and more action-packed, the fight scenes are louder and more violent, and the stunts are more grandiose. They are very formulaic: the hero's heroic and leads the narrative, there's a buddy (who turns into a rival or enemy), there's love interest, etc.

The movies are also very macho, with the emphasis completely on masculinity, on guys with guns, with the heroes trying to defend their masculine identities from all sorts of social and psychological as well as physical attacks.

Finally, interpretations of Phil Dick's fiction are not really adaptions, because they add so much to the stories (especially the short stories), altering them nearly beyond recognition. They have the kudos of being Dick adaptions, but, like so much of contemporary Hollywood's approach to literary properties, they take the story elements only as a starting-point: then they do what the hell they like.

Nothing wrong with that: it's what a movie should do, Orson Welles reckoned. A movie isn't a book or a piece of literature. Welles' approach to adapting books was to treat the text as part of the collaboration, but not something to be treated reverentially. Often, Welles used the text as a starting-point, a source of inspiration, but wound up departing from it (as in *The Lady From Shanghai*). Welles did not stick reverentially to the letter, the word and the text; he said he felt free to go in any direction he wished.[21]

Orson Welles railed against those critics who demanded that a film be 'faithful' to the original text by reproducing it in its entirety. Welles used the example of Giuseppe Verdi making operas out of William Shakespeare's plays many times as an illustration: 'when Verdi wrote *Falstaff* and *Otello*, nobody criticized *him* for radically changing Shakespeare' (2002, 132). Unfortunately, the additions and alterations to some of the Philip K. Dick movies are so extreme, they might as well not bother buying the rights to the material in the first place.[22]

21 'I don't believe in an essential reverence for the original material. It's simply part of the collaboration', Welles asserted (2002, 201).
22 The rights to Phil Dick's material have risen sharply from the 2,000 bucks that Brian Kelly paid for *Do Androids Dream of Electric Sheep?* in the 1970s.

RECIPE FOR A PHILIP K. DICK MOVIE

The typical Philip Kindred Dick movie contains the following ingredients:

▸ a hero who's hunted down for reasons he doesn't wholly understand;

▸ he has a loving wife/ girlfriend who stands by him, but he can't get back to her (the Dick films are always thoroughly heterosexual – and white American, too);

▸ there's a stern father figure;

▸ a mean villain;

▸ a sidekick or buddy;

▸ the government is corrupt and all-pervasive, close to fascist;

▸ the society is more brutal, the police more sadistic;

▸ a bunch of misfits or rebels band together to oppose the regime;

▸ even when the government and its agents seem to be on the side of what's good and right, they are still portrayed as suspect;

▸ and the hero gets the girl at the end and saves the world, but there's a price.

Other rules for a Philip K. Dick adaption include:

▸ there's always a scene with the hero on the run at night in rainswept city streets, backlit in blue;

▸ there's always an interrogation scene (with some hi-tech device);

▸ there's always a scene where a building or person is scanned or x-rayed;

▸ there's always some strange new drug;

▸ there're always some hi-tech environments which're contrasted with poor districts;

▸ there're always scenes with vidphones, screens, and surveillance;

▸ there's always a scene where some friend or colleague betrays the hero;

▸ there's always a scene where the hero has some crazy mind-reading, brain-altering machine strapped to his head;

▶▶ there are always machines which become like humans, and technology which goes awry.

Many Phil Dick movies are taken from short stories, and few from full-length novels – that inevitably means thousands of elements are added, such as new characters, action beats, gadgets, more back-story, more exposition, etc. Sometimes the films of Dick's fiction bear only a meagre resemblance to the original texts: the filmmakers will retain some key scenes, but go off in many different directions.

Finally, Philip K. Dick movie adaptions tend to be mounted as visual effects extravaganzas. *Blade Runner* began all that, with some extraordinary visual effects,[23] and films such as *Total Recall* and *Screamers* continued to put vfx at the centre of the movie. If you've got those sorts of visual effects in a film, that automatically increases the budget considerably. By the time of the pictures of the 2000s – *Minority Report, Paycheck, Next* – the visual effects budgets ran into tens of millions. And even more modest films, such as *Screamers* or *A Scanner Darkly*, are packed with visual effects.

So Philip K. Dick movies share many elements, from the big star parts for men, to the futuristic settings, to the elaborate look and design, to the visual effects. There are numerous ways of adapting a science fiction text, or of adapting Phil Dick's fiction, but, thus far, the Dick adaptions produced have been within a narrow set of formal, economic and cultural boundaries.

---

23 Originally budgeted by EEG at $5.5 million, the effects were cut down to $2 million.

THE DYSTOPIAS OF PHILIP K. DICK'S CINEMA

> If I can make you see the world the way I see it, then you will automatically think the way I think. You will come to the conclusions that I come to. And the greatest power one human being can exert over others is to control their perceptions of reality, and infringe on the integrity and individuality of their world.

Philip K. Dick[24]

Dystopian or apocalyptic visions of the future in sci-fi films, many of them post-nuclear or post-holocaust films, are so commonplace they're practically the default setting for sci-fi cinema. *Blade Runner* is a key movie of the dystopian type (but did dystopia ever look so compelling with its neons, skyscrapers, rain and post-punk design?). Dystopian sci-fi films include: *THX-1138* (1970), *Ice* (1970), *Glen and Randa* (1971), *The Ultimate Warrior* (1975), *A Boy and His Dog* (1975), *Damnation Alley* (1977), from Robert Zelazny's 1969 book, *Logan's Run* (1976), *The Final Programme* (1975), based on Michael Moorcock's Sixties *James Bond* parody, *The Last Battle* (1984), *Waterworld* (1995), *The Terminator* (1984), *A Clockwork Orange* (1972), based on Anthony Burgess's early Sixties novel, *The Lathe of Heaven* (1980), based on Ursula K. Le Guin's 1971 novel, *Millennium* (1989), *The Handmaid's Tale* (1990), based on Margaret Atwood's novel, *Sleeper* (1973), *Zardoz* (1974), *The Man Who Fell to Earth* (1976), *Escape From New York* (1981), *Escape From L.A.* (1996), *The Postman* (1997), *Westworld* (1973), *Deathrace 2000* (1975), *Rollerball* (1975), *Judge Dredd* (1995), *Twelve Monkeys* (1995), *Warlords* (1986), *Mutant Hunt* (1987), *Crime Zone* (1988), *Tin Star Void* (1989), *Welcome To Oblivion* (1990), *Roller Blade* (1986), *Cyborg* (1989), *MindWarp* (1992), *Ultra Warrior* (1993) and the *Mad Max* movies. Japanese *animé* movies and TV shows have delivered the most amazing dystopian fantasies: *Akira* (1988), *Ghost In the Shell* (1995, 2004), and *Legend of the Overfiend* (1989 onwards).

Films such as *A Scanner Darkly* and *Minority Report*

---

24 Quoted in C. Platt, 150.

are not as dystopic as *Blade Runner,* but there are serious things wrong with the contemporary American societies depicted in them. In *A Scanner Darkly* much of contemporary America is addicted to mind-altering drugs, while in *Minority Report* the government is covering up corruption that begins inside the legal and criminal system but by implication involves the wider society.

The animal subplot of *Blade Runner,* which was part of Hampton Fancher's script but is included only in the edges of *Blade Runner,* is part of science fiction's long-standing exploration of ecological issues (Philip K. Dick has explored ecological themes). Ecological concerns in sci-fi films include *The Omega Man* (1971), about biological warfare, *Z.P.G.* (1972) and *Soylent Green* (1973), about over-population[25] and *No Blade of Grass* (1970), based on John Christopher's *The Death of Grass* (1956). Concerns about the environment and ecology recurred in the 1990s, with films such as *Outbreak* (1995), *Twelve Monkeys* (1995), *The Stand* (1994), and *Princess Mononoke* (1997), and also some of the cycle of disaster movies of the same mid-1990s period.

25 Based on Harry Harrison's *Make Room! Make Room!*

BLADE RUNNER

BLADE RUNNER, STAR WARS AND *ALIEN*

I found *Star Wars* totally amazing when I saw it with friends in the English Midlands way back when. Beginning with the opening crawl and the view of the giant spaceship... Wow! Of course, scale and size ain't nuttin' new in movies: go back to 1916 and have a look at *Intolerance*, possibly the biggest American movie ever.[26] The scale of the imagery in *Intolerance* is so stupendous you *simply can't believe it.*

Many filmmakers, as well as fans and audiences, have raved about *Star Wars* and the effect it had on them when they first saw it in 1977. Ridley Scott, director of *Blade Runner*, recalled the impression that *Star Wars* had on him: 'frankly I couldn't believe it... this film was massive. It actually changed my mind about what I would do next'.[27] Scott said that seeing *Star Wars* was one of the reasons he decided to make *Alien* instead of the more highbrow *Tristan and Isolde*, to go for entertainment instead of something esoteric. Scott's version of *Dune*, he admitted, would be *very* much in the *Star Wars* vein.

> *Star Wars* is a great movie [enthused Scott]. It's abso-
> lutely extraordinary. Completely turned me around. I
> thought, "What the hell am I doing?" It's just the idea
> of taking that as a subject and doing it in a particular
> way was absolutely incredible. I never go to a film
> twice but I saw *Star Wars* four times, and I just

---

26 But not the grandest spectacle internationally – that is probably the Russian *War and Peace* of 1967.
27 In T. Shone, 86.

thought that all the detail was incredible.[28]

As *Star Wars* influenced *Blade Runner* (and *Alien*), so *Blade Runner* would in turn influence the later *Star Wars* films. The downtown area of Coruscant in 2002's *Star Wars: Attack of the Clones*, for instance, with its neons and Asians, resembles *Blade Runner* (as well as the cities in *Total Recall* and *Fifth Element*).[29]

Cultural theory critics seriously discussed the use of the replicants in *Blade Runner* in relation to racial and minority issues, but *Star Wars* was not given the same hallowed treatment, and was thought to be on the wrong side of racism. *Blade Runner* might be just as reactionary and right-wing (and plain dumb) as *Star Wars*, but for some cultural critics, *Star Wars* just wasn't as 'cool' as *Blade Runner*. *Blade Runner* had a cool, post-punk, postmodern sheen which snooty, snobby cultural theorists adore (plus it was a lesser-known movie, with its own cult of followers). But *Star Wars* was loud, silly, superficial entertainment for the masses.

ALIEN.

Alien was essentially a 1950s horror B-movie given an A-list sci-fi treatment, with hi-tech visual effects masking the fact that it was just another horror film about a monster terrorizing a group of people, as Ridley Scott admitted. This was true of other genre reworkings by the New Hollywood 'movie brat' filmmakers: *Close Encounters* updated the 1950s UFO and Cold War paranoia movie; *Jaws* was simply a Roger Corman monster flick with a bigger budget; and *Star Wars* was *Flash Gordon*. *Jaws* was definitely an influence on *Alien* – *Alien* was dubbed '*Jaws* in space', and Scott and his team often referred to *Jaws*, such as not showing the monster too much. David Giler called *Alien* 'a nasty *Star*

---

28 R. Scott, *Cinefantasique*, 12, 5-6, 1982.
29 *Attack of the Clones* shows off the new digital technology, though: instead of layers of film compiled in the optical printer as in *Blade Runner*, the second film of the second *Star Wars* trilogy shows off the ability of computerization to create three-dimensional images, enabling the high speed chase through the skyscrapers of Coruscant.

Wars'.30

The *Alien* films were made by 20th Century Fox, and had the continuity of being sci-fi adventures set in space or on distant planets, with a central character, Ellen Ripley, battling against evil alien creatures. However, each picture was created by a different team, and each was conceived to stand on their own (like most sequels). *Alien* looked back to Fifties sci-fi movies such as *It! The Terror From Beyond Space* (1958), *Them*, and also the low-budget *Planet of the Vampires* (Mario Bava, 1965).

BLADE RUNNER IN THE MARKETPLACE

The previews of *Blade Runner* were disastrous. The film was deemed too confusing, too slow, with too much going on visually.31 The story really is straightforward, but director Ridley Scott acknowledged that there were too many distractions in the look of the piece.32 So *Blade Runner* was another of thousands of movies which have been altered after previews.

Blade Runner grossed $27 million in the United States, placing it no. 16 in that year's box office chart (it was released on June 25, 1982, in 1,290 theatres in the U.S.A. – for the time, and still today, that's a very wide release). 1982 was the year, of course, of *E.T.*33 The films that came in way behind Steven Spielberg's Universal fantasy were *Tootsie* at

30 Some of the production team on *Alien* had worked on *Star Wars* (such as John Mollo, wardrobe, and designers Roger Christian and Les Dilley). *Alien* was also made at Fox, with Alan Ladd, Jnr OK-ing the film, the same executive who had green-lit *Star Wars*. The Ladd company invested $7.5m in *Blade Runner*.

31 The head honchos of Tandem didn't like the film at all: 'this movie gets worse with every screening,' they complained (M. Deeley, 2008, 251). They didn't like the voiceover, the stick figures, the slow pace, scenes that went on too long, and the weird bits.

32 One of the reasons for adding a voiceover was to clarify things for the audience (FN, 388).

33 Michael Deeley reckoned that audiences might be ready for something darker and less lightweight after *E.T.* (FN, 317), but that Summer was totally dominated by *E.T.* Indeed, *E.T.* took 10% of the total market share in 1982.

I don't agree that *E.T.* is lightweight and sentimental – *Blade Runner* is easily as sentimental, as conservative, as silly. But it has that 'dark', stylish veneer which seduces cultural critics into thinking they're looking at something Important and Worthy.

no. 2, *An Officer and a Gentleman* third, and *Rocky 3* in fourth place. Other sci-fi and fantasy flicks in 1982 included *Star Trek 2, Conan the Barbarian, Mad Max 2* and *The Thing*. *Blade Runner* is often trotted out as another big, important picture that flopped on its theatrical release. That isn't quite true, but it certainly wasn't a hit movie by any standards. The opening weekend was pretty good, but the movie seemed to fade away rapidly after that.

Many reviewers and critics came out against *Blade Runner* on its first release, including Roger Ebert, Pauline Kael, Sheila Benson, and Janet Maslin. 'Muddled', 'gruesome', 'pretentious' and 'overheated' were some of the words used to describe it.

RIDLEY SCOTT

As well as hundreds of commercials,[34] Ridley Scott (born in 1937 in South Shields in Tyne & Wear, Northern England) had also directed TV shows such as BBC's *Z-Cars* and *The Informer*. 'I was a designer trained as a painter, then an art director, and then from art direction drifted into graphic design', Scott explained (in H. Lightman, 1982). Scott has married twice (Felicity Heywood, 1964-1975, and Sandy Watson, 1979-1989), and has three children (Jake, Luke and Jordan).[35] More recently his partner has been actress Giannina Facio.

The movies directed by Ridley Scott can be grouped into genres: contemporary thrillers (*Black Rain, Someone To Watch Over Me, Hannibal, Body of Lies*); prestige historical films (*Gladiator, 1492, Robin Hood*); sci-fi and fantasy (*Alien, Legend* and *Blade Runner*); and the military is the *milieu* for many movies: *G.I. Jane, Black Hawk Down, Kingdom of Heaven, The Duellists* and others. Scott's films

34 Ridley Scott filmed the famous Hovis bread ad of the 1970s (in Shaftesbury in Dorset), and the pricey commercial for Apple, drawing on *1984* and Big Brother, in the 1980s.
35 Jake and Luke Scott have worked in their dad's business, and all three Scott kids are commercials directors (which's *very* unusual – for one kid to follow in a parents' footsteps is quite common, but not all three). Jake has directed a movie, *Plunkett & Macleane* (1999).

tend to be masculine and macho and rather grim,[36] headed up by big male stars: Harrison Ford, Michael Douglas, Denzel Washington, Leonardo di Caprio, Nic Cage, Gérard Depardieu and Russell Crowe (Crowe's now practically Scott's alter ego on screen). The involvement of Hollywood stars like that inevitably shapes the scripts. Both Dustin Hoffman and Harrison Ford changed the screenplay for *Blade Runner*, for instance.

Going to Hollywood has been common among British filmmakers from the 1910s onwards. Britain and Australia constituted the largest portion of filmmakers going to Hollywood (Charlie Chaplin, Alfred Hitchcock, and James Whale are famous examples in the classic Hollywood era). Since the decline of the British film industry in the late 1960s (partly due to American companies withdrawing their investment in British movies), British directors have been the most numerous imports into Hollywood: Guy Hamilton, J. Lee Thompson, John Schlesinger, Karel Reisz, Tony Richardson, Peter Yates and John Boorman in the 1960s; in the 1980s, Alan Parker, Ridley and Tony Scott, Michael Apted, Ken Russell, Mick Jackson, John Mackenzie, Jonathan Lynn, Stephen Frears, Neil Jordan, Adrian Lyne and Hugh Hudson.[37]

Filmmakers such as Alan Parker, Hugh Hudson, Adrian Lyne, Roland Joffé, Ridley Scott and Tony Scott had no qualms about going 'commercial', about aiming for big budget feature filmmaking in the American style. Parker, Lyne, Hudson and the Scotts were the film directors that did much of their groundwork in making TV adverts. Whether they made their movies in Britain (such as Ridley Scott's *Alien* or Alan Parker's *The Wall*), the product was distinctly American. Virtually all of Tony Scott's films are American, in

---

36 Comedy and humour are not Ridley Scott's strong points in movies, but that's also true of many pictures by his contemporaries, such as James Cameron, Steven Spielberg, George Lucas, etc (and many blockbuster and action-adventure movies). Scott's signature pics – *Alien, Gladiator, Thelma & Louise* and *Blade Runner* – tend to be rather serious and dour. And is there a single intentional piece of humour in *Blade Runner*? You have to think hard to find one. (That's down to the writers, however, and the producers, not necessarily the director. However, when you consider Scott's cinema as a whole, there are *very* few laughs).

37 Australian directors in Hollywood include Peter Weir, Bruce Beresford, George Miller, Philip Noyce and Fred Schepisi.

either feel, theme, location, finance or actors.

Some went to Hollywood earlier than others: Ridley Scott, for instance, went the Hollywood route right from the beginning, from his first film, *The Duellists* (1977), which, although some of it was shot in the U.K., had American stars (Keith Carradine and Harvey Keitel), and American money. Scott didn't make any movies with a 'British' subject for decades. Tony Scott followed his brother to Hollywood, producing American-style films from the beginning: *The Hunger, Beverly Hills Cop, Days of Thunder, Top Gun* and *The Last Boy Scout*. (The Scotts have a company, Scott Free, and have invested in British film studios – Shepperton, as well as producing TV shows such as *Numb3rs* and *The Good Wife*).

Ridley Scott followed up *Blade Runner* with his 20th Century Fox fairy tale film *Legend* (1985), a truly dreadful movie starring Tom Cruise, Mia Sara and Tim Curry. In *Legend*, Scott's, Assheton Gordon's and Alex Thomson's elaborate visuals this time really do smother the story, and *Legend*'s difficult to watch even once.[38] Go and rent *The Wizard of Oz* or anything by Hayao Miyazaki instead. ('I'll never want to do another movie like that again,' remarked Tom Cruise).[39]

Until 2000, Ridley Scott's biggest box office successes had been *Alien* and *Thelma & Louise*; he has his place assured in cinema history, by making two cult films: *Alien* and *Blade Runner*. Then, in 2000, *Gladiator* was released, and became no. 27 in a list of top grossing films at the worldwide box office (up until 2000), generating $440.9m. Made in conjunction with DreamWorks and Universal, it was the no. 2 earner of 2000 (behind *Mission: Impossible 2*).[40]

If Ridley's Scott's star languished somewhat in the mid-1990s (remember *1492: Conquest of Paradise* and *G.I. Jane*

---

38 The best thing about *Legend* is the soundtrack by German electronic gurus Tangerine Dream; in Europe *Legend* has a music track by Jerry Gold-smith.

39 T. Cruise, in C. Connelly, *Rolling Stone*, June 19, 1986.

40 Aside from being produced by DreamWorks, there are other links between *Gladiator* and Steven Spielberg: it was co-written by David Franzoni, who had authored *Amistad*; and it starred *Amistad*'s Djimon Hounsou, who played one of Russell Crowe's gladiator buddies.

anybody?),[41] it was revived big time with 2000's *Gladiator*, a reworking by David Franzoni, John Logan and William Nicholson of the ancient world historical epic (and virtually a remake of both *The Fall of the Roman Empire* and *Spartacus*). No Oscar for best director, but *Gladiator* won best film.

And from *Gladiator* onwards, Ridley Scott has been amazingly productive: *Black Hawk Down*, *A Good Year*, *Hannibal*, *Body of Lies*, *Kingdom of Heaven*, *American Gangster*, *Matchstick Men* and *Robin Hood*. Hell, that's about a movie a year! And by this time Scott wasn't young (he was 63 in 2000).

Following *Blade Runner*, Ridley Scott didn't make another movie as influential or as passionately admired as the 1982 Warners flick: his biggest success post-*Blade Runner* was probably *Thelma & Louise* and *Gladiator*. Certainly, films such as *White Squall*, *Black Rain*, *1492* and *Someone to Watch Over Me* had some of the impressive Ridley Scott visual style, but lacked the power of *Blade Runner*.

1996's *White Squall* is among my favourite of the movies that Ridley Scott has directed. It was an adventure film (based on a true story), concerning a group of teenage boys, part of the Ocean Academy, who set sail in 1961 around the world in the *Albatross*, a square-rigged Brigantine, accompanied by an English teacher (John Savage) who spouts lines of William Shakespeare (the opening of *The Tempest* being the inevitable first bit of the Bard quoted in the film), and the tough, determined, charismatic skipper, Christopher Sheldon (Jeff Bridges).

The themes here were the relations between fathers and sons, men and boys, with Jeff Bridges as the 'good father' (strong, dynamic, but also fair), and the 'bad father', the rich man who overwhelms his child with a possessive love. Uneasy relations between fathers and sons are recurring themes in Scott's cinema.

White Squall was a strangely reactionary and simplistic film, the characters easily recognizable stereotypes: the

41 *G.I. Jane* is one of those films you forget instantly as soon as you've seen it. Demi Moore with a shaved head doing press-ups I remember, but little else.

tough, silent captain; the ship bully who hides an insecurity about his lack of education; the boy scared of heights (his brother died when falling from a tree). The speech made by the film's narrator, the youth at the centre of the teenage group of boys, summarized the movie's thrust: it was about boy's and men's stuff, yet another Hollywood film about fathers and sons, with sons doing the things they had to do, and fathers doing the things they had to do. The film ended with a group hug, the boys surrounding the weeping captain in the courtroom (these scenes were overlong).

In the portraits of the captain and his relation with the boys who admired him and would have followed him anywhere, one sensed the relation Ridley Scott himself is said to have had with his film crews, actors and even his own children (Scott's son Jake spoke of elements of his father in his film characters in a BBC TV *Omnibus* interview). But for all its faults, *White Squall* is still an engaging and enjoyable piece.

Black Hawk Down (2001) I find disturbing for its unashamedly gung-ho and uncritical pro-American, right-wing politics (and it's also ridiculously, grotesquely violent).[42] I have friends like James Smith who disagree with me completely about *Black Hawk Down*. For me, *Black Hawk Down* is virtually an advert for the American military machine, and could not have been made, like *Top Gun* (which Scott's brother Tony directed for Don Simpson and Jerry Bruckheimer), without the full co-operation of the US military. Talk about increasing co-operation between Washington and Hollywood: *Black Hawk Down* was a movie as a war machine.

Hannibal (2001), part of the *Silence of the Lambs/* Thomas Harris franchise, was overseen by film legend Dino de Laurentiis (1919-2010), for whom Ridley Scott had worked on the abandoned *Dune* project. *Hannibal* was a pitifully bad thriller, woefully misjudged in tone and substance. It's difficult to believe that Ridley Scott directed

---

42 Of *Black Hawk Down*, Joe Morgenstern wrote: 'Functions mainly as an action extravaganza, and a numbingly depersonalized one at that' (*Wall Street Journal*). 'It's every bit as harrowing – and also every bit as pointless and misguided – as the botched military mission it depicts', remarked Andrew O'Hehir in Salon.com.

it, and that David Mamet and Steve Zallian worked on the screenplay (*Steve Zallian*! He wrote *Schindler's List*! Much-celebrated playwright *David Mamet*!).[43]

According to Wikipedia, the budget for *Hannibal* was $87 million. 87,000,000 bucks! You have GOT to be kidding! For a routine thriller that would cost less than a million on TV! ($200,000 if you're Roger Corman!).

For everyone concerned, *Hannibal* is lamentable.[44] But we should remember that *Hannibal* wasn't Ridley Scott's concept, or franchise, or characters, or script: the producers on *Hannibal* were L. Franco, B. Melniker, C. Roven and E. Thomas.

And the less said about *Kingdom of Heaven* (2005) the better. Some people enjoyed the film,[45] but have a look at *Hero, The House of Flying Daggers, The Curse of the Golden Flower* or *Seven Swordsmen*, big Chinese movies, to see how action-oriented historical films should be done in the contemporary era. Sure, the battles and the action were terrific in *Kingdom of Heaven*, but Orlando Bloom in the lead role had the charisma of a soggy cardboard box. Orlando Bloom! You gotta be kidding! Where's Arny?!

Simply dreadful: *Kingdom of Heaven* was completely a *producer's* movie, like almost every movie that comes out of Hollywood. Despite the enshrinement of the *auteur*, still at work in the marketing and PR of movies (and Ridley Scott is regularly trumpeted as an *auteur*), the American film industry is wholly producer-dominated. And you can see the involvement of producers and studio executives everywhere in *Kingdom of Heaven*. It's all so cynically calculated, like the rejuvenation of Warners' *Batman* franchise (with *Batman Begins*) in the same year, 2005: 'OK, we have a bit of martial arts business for this section of the audience, some romance, a mentor figure who dies', and so on.

---

43 Some critics agree with me: 'very likely the worst film of this year and quite possibly the next', commented Charles Taylor in Salon.com, while Ella Taylor in *LA. Weekly* called it 'the flabbiest of cop-outs'. Mick LaSalle in the *San Francisco Chronicle* found *Hannibal* 'wilfully gross, fundamentally stupid and in no way worth the discomfit of watching it.'

44 The stars were Anthony Hopkins, Julianne Moore, Ray Liotta and Gary Oldman.

45 And some critics didn't: 'muddled and oppressive storytelling' (Stephen Zacharek, Salon.com); 'a frustratingly thin epic' (Ian Nathan, *Empire*); 'fails to arouse any passion' (David Denby, *Newsweek*).

One critical view of the films directed by Ridley Scott is that they are slick, professional, beautiful to look at, but lacking in substance, with shallow characters.46 Another criticism is that Scott spends so much time on his visuals he ignores narrative; Scott, though, always stresses the script and the story. The most important part of his movies, Scott said, was the script. 'Yet the toughest part is also always the screenplay, every time. Movie-making is really all story, story, story' (P. Sammon, 1999, 132). Getting the script right first before shooting began was Scott's goal: sci-fi demands rigorous planning and pre-production, Scott said.

> Sci-fi presents a wonderful opportunity, because if you get it right, anything goes. But you'd better have drawn up your rule book for the world you've created first. Then you'd better stick to it. (FN, 380)

BLADE RUNNER AND 2001: A SPACE ODYSSEY

For many, including myself, *2001: A Space Odyssey* is *the* great sci-fi movie (other classics or favourites might include *Solaris, Forbidden Planet, Metropolis, Alien, Ghost In the Shell, Akira, Nausicäa of the Valley of the Wind, Close Encounters of the Third Kind* and *Star Wars*).

2001: A Space Odyssey was an immensely influential film; the 1968 picture, with its combination of technology and the mystical, the future and otherness, did not just influence most of the sci-fi movies that followed (such as *Dark Star, Silent Running, Logan's Run, Black Hole*, the *Star Trek* TV series, *Star Trek: The Motion Picture, Contact,* the *Star Wars* series, *Close Encounters of the Third Kind,* the *Terminator* films, *The Abyss,* the *Alien* series and some of the *James Bond* outings [such as *Moonraker*]), it also influenced the way science was presented on TV and radio.

MGM's epic film inaugurated the era of wonder and awe at the universe, which directly led to some of the most

46 Others have accused Scott's films of a sometimes misanthropic world-view, and a dubious portrayal of women. For a tiny fraction of further negative criticism of Scott's cinema, see M. Garrone, Salon.com; Jim Moran, Lost In Negative Space, 2006, and Joshua Tyler, Cinema-Blend.com, 2006.

lucrative (sci-fi) movies – *Close Encounters, E.T., Star Trek, Star Wars* – and the way space and sci-fi would be depicted with slow or grand music, or in long, meditative shots (yup, including the opening sequence of *Blade Runner*). Twenty years later, during the anniversary celebrations of the moon landings, the space scenes were still being accompanied by mysterious music (this time by Brian Eno and Harold Budd); thirty years later, for the BBC's *The Planets* TV series, this sort of approach was still being employed (this time with swathes of post-Vangelis synthesizer).[47]

References to *2001: A Space Odyssey* popped up in odd places: in pop promos by Lenny Kravitz, the Thompson Twins and Michael Jackson (John Landis, who directed the *Thriller* music video, liked to include the line 'see you next Wednesday', spoken by Poole's parents, in all his films). Woody Allen's movies alluded to *2001: A Space Odyssey* – *Sleeper* and *Manhattan,* for example (Allen had at first disliked the film, then came round to appreciating it). Jan de Bont put Kubrick films in his own films: *2001: A Space Odyssey* is seen in *Speed,* and *The Shining* in *Twister.*

Some filmmakers after *2001: A Space Odyssey* deliberately designed their films in opposition to the clean, efficient world it depicted: movies such as *Alien, Blade Runner* and *Star Wars* went the other way, creating a messy, disorganized future world. George Lucas said he didn't want his spaceships to look like the ones in *2001: A Space Odyssey,* too neat and tidy, while the *Nostromo* in *Alien* went even further in designer chaos and shadows.

An important aspect of *2001: A Space Odyssey* is the relation it re-established (and developed) between movies and the concept of the 'sublime'. In painting, that means the sublime in landscape painters such as J.M.W. Turner and John Martin, with their grand visions of mountains and ancient civilizations, up to the 'Abstract Sublime' of the Abstract Expressionists, in particular Barnett Newman and Mark Rothko, who made huge canvases of single colours, or two or three hues combined. Theirs was a self-consciously

47 Even thirty years and more after its release its influence could still be discerned – in *Mission To Mars,* for example, directed by one-time 'movie brat' Brian de Palma, or the *Solaris* remake of 2002. Or in many Japanese animations.

religious art, deliberately mythic and heroic, with transcendent, timeless and tragic subject matter. Their art culminated in the enormous, austere and very dark paintings in the Rothko Chapel in Houston, and Newman's ascetic *Stations of the Cross* series. The more 'sublime' reaches of Abstract Expressionism have a melodramatic, operatic quality, which seems to be reaching for something it is not equipped either to grasp or to put to use. It is an art of striving or Nietzschean 'becoming', and this journey towards transcendence sometimes produces paintings that are so self-consciously 'sublime', 'epic' and 'heroic' that they fall into bathos or fascism (criticisms that have been made of Stanley Kubrick and *2001: A Space Odyssey*).

The sublime had always been a part of cinema (from early films such as *Intolerance* onwards), but after *2001: A Space Odyssey*, it became an essential ingredient of sci-fi and fantasy films (think of *Star Wars, Close Encounters of the Third Kind, Blade Runner, Total Recall, Independence Day* and *The Fifth Element*). *2001: A Space Odyssey* set the precedent for the sublime in sci-fi films, for gigantic scale, infinite distances, mysteries, long, elaborate shots, and complex special effects.

A sense of wonder is one of the hallmarks of science fiction, and *2001: A Space Odyssey* trades on producing awe throughout many sections: every time the monolith appears (in prehistory, at the Tycho site, in Jupiter space and in the 18th century room); during the whole end section (from the Jupiter space scenes, through the Stargate, to the 18th century room and the final Star Child images); and in most of the space flight scenes.

For at least half of *2001: A Space Odyssey*, then, the filmmakers are reaching towards the manufacture of amazement, with the viewer required to be in a state of awe. *2001: A Space Odyssey* is literally meant to be one of sci-fi's 'amazing stories', emphatically 'astounding' (to use two famous sci-fi magazine titles). And *Blade Runner*, although super-cynical with its crime/ detective/ hard-boiled genre elements, also works hard to evoke awe and wonder.

2001: A Space Odyssey doesn't take place in a future dystopia, with society falling apart; rather, *2001: A Space*

Odyssey offers a rare example of a democratic, functioning future society (or, at least, in America, and America's outposts in space and on the moon). However, from the late 1960s onwards, there were far more films portraying a dystopian vision of the future, of societies in the process of crumbling, from the ecological and disaster films of the 1970s, to the post-apocalyptic nuclear wastelands of the 1980s.

Again, one sees how *2001: A Space Odyssey* is born out of the optimism, politically, socially and technologically, of the early-to-mid-1960s. If *2001: A Space Odyssey* had been conceived in the late 1960s or early 1970s, it would probably have shown a different picture of the future. Sci-fi films of disasters, viruses and ecological failures started appearing from the late 1960s (and especially the early 1970s) onwards (*The Andromeda Strain, Westworld, The Omega Man, Planet of the Apes, Silent Running, Soylent Green, Rollerball* and *THX-1138*, for example).[48] Indeed, Stanley Kubrick's next film would be about this very subject – *A Clockwork Orange* – with the familiar dystopian themes of a totalitarian state, urban wastelands, brainwashing, ultra-violence, alienation, and so on.

Politically, *Blade Runner* wants to have it both ways, both utopian and dystopian: it wants to be a cool, distanced look at contemporary North America, with cynical characters and hard-boiled attitudes, an America where the idealism of the 1960s is long forgotten. Yet *Blade Runner* is also, like *Star Wars* and many sci-fi and fantasy films of the period, distinctly rightwing and pro-American (the term often used is 'Reaganite').[49]

Blade Runner depicts the late capitalist society of the Eighties exaggerated: the 'haves' are fewer and have more, while the 'have nots' are poorer and more numerous (and are of non-white, Western origin). The middle-classes have migrated to the suburbs (the Off-world colonies), while the poor and immigrants live in over-crowded streets and apartment blocks, right next to derelict or empty buildings (such as J.F. Sebastian's).

48 The look of George Lucas's first feature film, *THX 1138*, derived very much from *2001: A Space Odyssey*.
49 Most of Ridley Scott's films tend to be pro-military and pro-America.

STANLEY KUBRICK.

The number of film directors who've been influenced by Stanley Kubrick, or who acknowledge him as one of the masters, is many: Ridley Scott (*2001: A Space Odyssey*'s influence can be seen in *Alien* and *Blade Runner*, *Spartacus* in *Gladiator*, and *Barry Lyndon* on Scott's first film, *The Duellists*; Scott even made his own version of *Paths of Glory*, in the early 1960s); John Carpenter's *Dark Star* was (partly) a *2001* spoof; James Cameron claimed that *2001* was one of the reasons he became a director; François Truffaut's *Vivement Dimance!* featured *Paths of Glory*; Michael Mann said he would have loved to have made *Dr Strangelove* (if he remade it, he wouldn't change a thing); and Quentin Tarantino's *Reservoir Dogs* (1992) reworks *The Killing*.

BLADE RUNNER AND SOLARIS

Russian filmmaker Andrei Tarkovsky (1932-86) produced a version of Stanislaw Lem's novel *Solaris* in 1972 for Mosfilm. Often referred to as the 'Russian *2001*' (Tarkovsky wasn't keen on the 1968 Hollywood film), *Solaris* explores similar territory to *Blade Runner*, but in a much more impressive way in many respects.

There are obvious affinities between the replicas in *Solaris* and the replicants in *Blade Runner*. *Blade Runner*'s replicants have been likened by film critics to different ethnic minorities; marginalized, they have to live off the planet; the police boss Bryant refers to them as 'skin jobs', evoking the racist policemen in other films referring to 'niggers'.[50] The replicants are slaves, and work in the 'Off-World colonies', recalling the slave trade of the West. For some critics, the replicants are at the centre of *Blade Runner*'s exploration of reality and dream, the imagined and the real past, real and implanted memories, themes which are reflected in the tensions between the modernist and

50 In subsequent years, the term 'nigger' would assume even greater strength as a term of racial hatred, while also being taken up hip-hop artists as a positive word.

postmodern look of the film, its 'retrofitting', the evocation of the future using elements of the past.

The themes of time, mortality, memory and reality/artifice are taken up in the photographs the replicants collect (in *Solaris*, as in most of Andrei Tarkovsky's films, paintings, rather than photographs, are the psychic touchstone, indicating Tarkovsky's more traditional modernism, preferring painting over photography. But Tarkovsky does use photographs of Kris's mother, and of Hari, at key moments).

For Deckard in *Blade Runner*, the photos are fakes provided by genetic engineering boss Tyrell to aid the implanted memories of the replicants, and thus control them (in a way, Kris, the hero of *Solaris,* uses the home videos he shows Hari as a way of humanizing her, of helping her to become more 'human'. It's as if he's educating her, rebuilding her).

Deckard also collects photographs, which are 19th and 20th century images, of people he could not have known personally, suggesting that these too are fakes. The photos are little pieces of history and the world, whether faked or not, and they are needed by humans or cyborgs to fill in missing gaps in their lives (in *Solaris*, one of the first things the mimoid Hari does is to study closely a photograph of the real Hari that Kris has brought with him).

In a totally postmodern world, where surface is everything, photographs (or home movies) may stand in for memories, may have as much weight and resonance as real memories. Much of *Blade Runner* concerns a nostalgia for 'real life', for something beyond mere image and surface, for something beyond the flashing, swivelling lights, the layers of rain and smoke, the huge wedding cake of artifice, an escape into reality; and always with the sense that time is running out – for Rachel as well as for the murderous replicants. 'Too bad she won't live', says Gaff at the end of the film, 'but then again, who does?'[51]

Like Deckard in *Blade Runner*, Kris in *Solaris* finds himself falling in love with a replica of a woman, something

51 Bryant was going to appear and say the line, but it made more sense to have Gaff do that, Katy Haber remarked, because Gaff had left the paper unicorn, and had been following Deckard around (FN, 198).

synthetic (half-human, half-cyborg in *Blade Runner*, and a woman made of neutrinos in *Solaris*), manufactured by a higher intelligence (the Tyrell Corporation and the Ocean). And, importantly, both Deckard and Kris begin not to care if the women they love are not 'real'; the *feelings* they have for them, the bonds between them, have more significance than their flesh-and-blood materiality. Also, both Rachel and Hari begin to ask questions about their origins and real selves, and Deckard and Kris muse on what is real and what isn't. The journey of both Deckard and Kris is to learn to become more human, more humane and compassionate.

Thus, although *Blade Runner* is a piece of mainstream Hollywood entertainment, it is also in the category of the metaphysical sci-fi film (of which *2001: A Space Odyssey* is the obvious example), though it is nowhere near as meditative and introspective as the Soviet classic.

THE SCRIPT AND PRE-PRODUCTION

I don't regard *Blade Runner*[52] as 'a Ridley Scott film', or a film which relies entirely for its success on one person, Ridley Scott. I've mentioned Scott a lot here, but *Blade Runner* is more a Philip K. Dick film, or a Hampton Fancher film, than it is a Ridley Scott film, in so many respects. Oh, of course Scott's involvement was critical to *Blade Runner,* but many of the things viewers love about the movie – the design, the *mise-en-scène,* the music, the romance – come from other sources: the design work of Lawrence Paull, Syd Mead, David Snyder, Moebius *et al*, Vangelis Papathanassiou's music, the cinematography of Jordan Cronenweth[53] and his team. And then there's the script, the script, the script – and that was by Hampton Fancher and David

---

52 I went to see *Blade Runner* at the ABC cinema in Bournemouth in October 1982, when I was studying at film school, and loved it, of course.
53 Prior to *Blade Runner,* Jordan Cronenweth had lit *Altered States*, a $15m sci-fi extravaganza directed by England's great visionary director, the utterly extraordinary Ken Russell.

Peoples (and Daryl Ponicsan and Roland Kibbee).[54]

Although most people credit Ridley Scott with creating much of the final film, Scott himself says the movie is really Fancher's ('my final impression was of how much of *Blade Runner* was Hampton Fancher's movie', Scott said when he saw the film on the BBC in 1995 [FN, 393]); most of the key personnel on the production rated Fancher's script highly ('the most driving and interesting and original piece of writing I'd ever seen', said Michael Deeley [FN, 34]). Fancher introduced a number of elements into the script, including an ecological slant (in the rarity of real animals).

Martin Scorsese had considered filming Philip K. Dick's novel *Do Androids Dream of Electric Sleep?* in 1969; he was going to buy it for Jay Cocks to write the script. Robert Jaffe (son of the producer Herb Jaffe) wrote the first script, in the mid-70s. Dick didn't like Jaffe's script at all: 'so terribly done I couldn't believe it was a shooting script', Dick remarked (FN, 23). Dick was suspicious of Hollywood, and the way it operated. He loved movies, but found Hollywood's way of doing things difficult to take.

The project passed to Hampton Fancher and producer Brian Kelly, who completed a screenplay in 1974, which Philip K. Dick disliked. Fancher had turned his book into a bunch of clichés about private detectives, Dick thought. (Fancher has few writing credits, and was mainly known as an actor: it's one of the amazing things about *Blade Runner* that this cult classic movie loved by millions wasn't penned by a Hollywood veteran, but by a young newcomer).

It wasn't *Blade Runner*, though, that made Philip Kindred Dick one of the cool writers in sci-fi for Hollywood, but the success of 1990's *Total Recall*. Screenwriter Ron Shusett had paid $1,000 for the option on Dick's "We Can Remember It For You Wholesale" in the 1970s, which *Total Recall* was based on; after *Total Recall*, Dick's estate was asking for $500,000 for stories of the same length. By 2002, a Dick story (*Minority Report*) was the basis for a picture made by two of Hollywood's biggest talents – Steven Spielberg and Tom Cruise.

54 The DVD release of *The Final Cut* of *Blade Runner* is worth having solely for the audio commentary by Fancher and Peoples, as they discuss the script in detail, and wonder who wrote what.

Barbara Hershey had helped to persuade Hampton Fancher to write the screenplay55 (Hershey had also tested for the part of Rachel).56 Producer Brian Kelly bought the rights to the 1968 book (for $2000!) and commissioned Fancher to write the script; Fancher had wanted to act as a producer, not writer, at first. Kelly persuaded him to have a go at writing the screenplay. Fancher preferred some of Dick's other stories to *Do Androids Dream of Electric Sheep?* But he did admire the paranoid, Kafkaesque quality of *Electric Sheep*, and liked the idea of doing the book as 'a chase movie, with a detective after androids in a dystopic world' (FN, 26).

Brian Kelly took the project to British producer Michael Deeley (who turned it down twice before being convinced).57 Deeley's producer credits included *The Italian Job, Murphy's War, The Wicker Man, Nickelodeon, Convoy, The Deer Hunter,* and *The Man Who Fell to Earth* (some of these became, like *Blade Runner*, cult films). Deeley said he had been attracted by the 'marvellous blending of a thriller with a romance,' in Hampton Fancher's script, and the moral drama of a cop falling for his quarry. David Peoples was called in by Scott and Deeley to revise Fancher's screenplay.58 Bringing in Peoples was very upsetting for Fancher at first, although he later appreciated Peoples' con-

55 Fancher said 'it was really Barbara Hershey who convinced me that writing a script was the only way to get this project off the ground' (FN, 31).
56 For me, Barbara Hershey would've been much more satisfying than Sean Young, who is, to put it kindly, not the most compelling of actresses. Maybe it helped in *Blade Runner* that Young was playing a robot – her rather blank, uninvolved style suited the part (Young was 22 at the time of filming, and had appeared in *Jane Austen In Manhattan* and *Stripes*).

Three actresses were screentested, including Young and Hershey (some say there were more). The filmmakers auditioned about 50 actresses for the part. Scott wanted Monique van den Ven, who had appeared in Paul Verhoeven's eccentric Seventies film *Turkish Delight*. One reason for not casting Hersey, for Deeley and Scott, was that she was too well-known.

For Pris the casting team screentested four actors, including Stacey Nelkin, who was cast as Mary, the mother android.
57 Fancher commented later that Kelly had kept the project alive, for the year it took to write the first draft (FN, 32).
58 David Peoples was then working for Scott's brother Tony, at Filmways. After *Blade Runner*, writer Peoples went on to script *Ladyhawke* (Richard Donner, 1985), a sword-and-sorcery romp with Rutger Hauer, Matthew Broderick and Michelle Pfeiffer, *Leviathan* (George Pan Cosmatos, 1989), a lame sci-fi film, *Predator* (John McTiernan, 1987), an Arnold Schwarzenegger action movie, *The Salute of the Jugger* (1990, a.k.a. *The Blood of Heroes*), which starred Rutger Hauer, and *Twelve Monkeys* (1995), one of the best post-*Blade Runner* sci-fi movies.

tribution to the piece. It was one of those situations where the writers hadn't met before Peoples started to revise Fancher's scripts. And after he'd been replaced, Fancher said he'd not kept up with the production, and stayed away (FN, 318).

Robert Mulligan was the first director attached to the project (for a time it looked like the film would be made with Mulligan and Universal). Later, CBS Films were in the running to make the movie, but they dropped out when the budget grew too big (partly due to Ridley Scott expanding the film's scope).

Dangerous Days (as *Blade Runner* was called then) had already been in the development stage for months before Ridley Scott came on board. Scott turned down *Blade Runner* when he was first offered it, despite Michael Deeley and Ivor Powell persuading him to do it. One reason was that Scott had recently finished a sci-fi flick (*Alien*), and wanted to explore other subjects. Another reason was he was already committed to Dino di Laurentiis' *Dune*.

(After the success of *Star Wars*, Ridley Scott was commissioned to make *Dune* for Dino de Laurentiis, and had developed a screenplay in 1981 with Rudy Wurlitzer (a former Sam Peckinpah collaborator, who had written *Pat Garrett and Billy the Kid* and the novel *Quake*). Artist H.R. Giger was brought in. Preparations commenced at Pinewood Studios. But Ridley Scott took on *Blade Runner*, when the budget for *Dune* escalated to $50m (and the script was rumoured to be exploring the theme of incest. Scott had initially declined making *Blade Runner*, because of *Dune*). Scott worked later for de Laurentiis on the sequel to *The Silence of the Lambs, Hannibal.*)

❀

Personnel on *Blade Runner* included producers Michael Deeley, Bud Yorkin, Jerry Perenchio and Brian Kelly; writers Hampton Fancher, David Peoples, Daryl Ponicsan and Roland Kibbee (Yorkin also contributed to the script); associate/ assistant producers Ivor Powell and Katy Haber; director Ridley Scott; DP Jordan Cronenweth; editors Terry Rawlings, William Zabala and Marsha Nakashima; hair by Shirley Padgett; make-up by Marvin Westmore and Bridget O'Neill;

production managers C.O. Erickson and John Rogers; assistant director Newt Arnold; props by Terry Lewis; art directors Stephen Dane and David Snyder; production designers Larry Paull and Peter Hampton; casting by Mike Fenton, Jane Feinberg and Marci Liroff; illustrators Tom Southwell and Syd Mead; sound by Bud Alper and Peter Pennell; script supervisor Ana Maria Quintana; visual effects by Doug Trumbull, David Dryer, and Richard Yuricich; matte paintings by Matthew Yuricich; stunts by Gary Combs and his team; wardrobe by Michael Kaplan and Charles Knode, with additional design by Moebius a.k.a. Jean Giraud (plus Winnie Brown, Bob Horn, James Lapidus, Linda Matthews, Jan Ferris and Jenny Herrin); and performers such as Harrison Ford, Rutger Hauer, Sean Young, Daryl Hannah, William Sanderson, Joe Turkel, M. Emmet Walsh, James Hong, Brion James, Morgan Paull, Joanna Cassidy and Edward Olmos James.

The initial budget of *Blade Runner* was $13.5 million; producer Michael Deeley negotiated a more expensive deal after Filmways (the original producers) pulled out: Warners and the Ladd Company put in $7.5 million; Tandem put in $7 million, for ancillary rights (including providing the completion bond);[59] Sir Run Run Shaw (of the famous Shaw Brothers in China)[60] put in $7.5 million, for foreign rights; the final budget of $21.5 million was raised to $28 million.[61] The effects cost $3.5 million for 90 shots. Paul Sammon called it the 'first $28 million mainstream science fiction art film' (1996, 7).[62] (While some have drawn attention to the high budget of *Blade Runner*, *Legend*, 3 years later, cost $30 million, and was a much bigger flop at the box office.

59 Including TV, home entertainment, cable, etc. Tandem also owned the negative.
60 Sir Run Run Shaw (1918-91) was one of the major movie moguls in China of recent times. The Shaw Brothers were the main distributors of American movies in China after WW2. With their studio in Hong Kong, they dominated Chinese cinema (at their peak, in 1966, the Shaws produced 40 movies. Their studio had 12 soundstages). Shaw Brothers moved into TV production in the 1970s. For ten or so years (from 1983-1995), they ceased film production, but resumed in 1995. The Shaws are still a key distributor in South-east Asia, and also hold many business interests, including theatres and real estate.
61 Thirteen Hollywood film companies turned *Blade Runner* down after Filmways bailed out, including Fox, United Artists and Universal (FN, 66).
62 Maybe; actually, *Solaris* and *2001: A Space Odyssey* were big budget science fiction art movies before *Blade Runner*.

$30 million bucks! What a shocking waste of $$$$$).

The title, *Blade Runner*, came from William Burroughs, who was a fan of Philip K. Dick's fiction (his *Blade Runner: A Movie* had reworked Alan Nourse's novel). The title was bought for a small fee; the production team also wanted to get rid of calling Deckard a detective, and of using the well-worn concept of androids (it was David Peoples and his daughter Risa who came up with the name replicants [FN, 61]).63

The film is set in 2019 because 2020 had connotations with vision ('20-20 vision'). After the awkward title *Do Androids Dream of Electric Sheep?* was shortened to *Android*,64 the film was called *Mechanismo,* then *Dangerous Days* for a long time. *Gotham City* was also considered by the filmmakers, but Bob Kane, the creator of *Batman*, wouldn't sell the name.

Katy Haber was one of the key personnel on *Blade Runner;* it was Haber who suggested casting Rutger Hauer, a vital decision (she recalled that she showed some of Hauer's movies which he'd made with Paul Verhoeven to the producers – *Turks Fruit, Keetje Tippel* and *Soldaat van Oranje* – and Hauer was cast, without meeting Ridley Scott [FN, 130]).

Jerry Perenchio and Bud Yorkin were part of Tandem, the production company; Tandem (linked to Embassy) was best-known for TV productions. Tandem is usually cast as the baddie in accounts of *Blade Runner*'s production, with the director Scott, producer Deeley, writers Fancher and Peoples, and some of the crew on the other side, the good side. Stories of *Blade Runner* pit the studio (Warners) and the production company (Tandem) against the filmmakers.65 It's never that simple, though.

---

63 For Dick, an android was a 'metaphor for people who are physiologically human but behaving in a nonhuman way' (FN, 16).

64 There's an odd, not particularly successful but kinda watchable movie called *Android*, which stars the inimitable Klaus Kinski (directed by Aaron Lipstadt in 1982).

65 Everyone has a different views of events on a troubled picture like this – their own agendas, their own memories. For instance, Tandem fired Michael Deeley and Ridley Scott, but that lasted about two weeks, during which time Deeley and Scott continued to work on the movie anyway. Editor Terry Rawlings recalled how he delayed Tandem re-cutting the film, by telling them it was in pieces and wasn't ready to be worked on as a whole (FN, 209).

The production needed Tandem and the $7 million they brought to the table. Without them, the film might not have been made at that time. The filmmakers probably would have preferred not to have given Tandem so much control, however, as Michael Deeley hinted in the documentary *Dangerous Days* (particularly of the complex post-production process).[66]

Incredibly, Ridley Scot admitted he hadn't been able to finish the book *Do Androids Dream of Electric Sheep?*. That's not going to endear an author to the people adapting their book, is it, if they haven't even bothered to read the thing all the way through?! (and Dick's books aren't particularly long – certainly not compared to some fantasy and sci-fi authors, who seem to think that 'epic' and 'grand' means writing books that are 800-pages plus).

Philip K. Dick had come out publicly against the film (it started way back, when Hampton Fancher had done the first adaption of the book), but he was won over when he came to a screening in L.A. to see some of the footage.

THE DIRECTOR'S CUT OF *BLADE RUNNER*

There are apparently six versions of *Blade Runner*, the main three being the 1982 version, the 1992 *Director's Cut*, and the 2007 *Final Cut*; the main differences between the first two are the loss of the hard-boiled detective voiceover, and the 'happy' ending.

The voiceover had been in the original script, but was taken out, before being put back in by the studio's executives. Ridley Scott and Harrison Ford were not happy with the voiceover; Scott had been impressed by Martin Sheen's voiceover in *Apocalypse Now*, and wanted it in *Blade Runner*, but he and his writers hadn't been able to nail it. It was Scott who pushed for the voiceover, according to

---

66 Scott said he didn't feel that he and Tandem were working on the same wavelength; they just couldn't quite understand the type of film he was trying to make. However, Scott also thought that the extra $3-4 million that Perenchio and Yorkin put into the movie on top of their $7 million, was probably 'a drop in the ocean for those guys' (FN, 386).

Hampton Fancher and others (FN, 292). 'We wrestled with it and wrestled with it', explained Scott, but they couldn't crack it (FN, 388). Voiceover, Scott reflected, 'is extremely difficult to pull off, because in a way it has to be totally internal and reflective' (ibid.). The voiceover was recorded three times in an effort to nail it (FN, 295).

As well as Peoples, Fancher, Yorkin and others, Daryl Ponicsan and Roland Kibbee also contributed to the voiceover. Some of the voiceovers were recorded after the picture was pretty much done and was being screened at sneak previews. A voiceover recording was added after the Dallas and Denver previews, for instance, overseen by Yorkin, Katy Haber and Kibbee.

The six versions are on video cassette, laser disc, DVD Blu-ray and theatrical release. Paul Sammon in *Future Noir*, the best book on *Blade Runner* (which I've drawn on a lot in my book), has made a detailed study of the differences between the versions.[67] Sammon defines the versions thus:

(1) the domestic (US) cut,

(2) the international cut (both 1982),

(3) the TV version (1986),

(4) Ridley Scott's *Director's Cut* (1992),

(5) the San Diego preview print (shown only once, in May, 1982),

(6) the workprint, shown at sneak previews in Denver and Dallas,

(7) and what Paul Sammon calls the Fairfax cut, the UCLA cut, and the NuArt/ Castro cut.[68]

Paul Sammon's book also details the many differences between each of the television, laser disc and video cassette versions. The broadcast version (for CBS, 1986) cut some of the language (for example, Batty tells Tyrell before he kills him 'I want more life, father', instead of 'I want more life,

---

67 In Appendix B.

68 On the 2007 home entertainment releases of the 'final cut' of *Blade Runner*, the deleted and alternate scenes were strung together with a voiceover by Harrison Ford, and constituted yet another version of *Blade Runner* (though not the entire story).

In this version of *Blade Runner*, the narration works nicely in relating Deckard's hunt for the replicants, enabling the deleted and alternative scenes to be put together in a logical sequence which's a satisfying alternative to the more well-known cuts of *Blade Runner*.

fucker');[69] there are widescreen versions, panned and scanned versions, and ones with different aspect ratios.

The video version to have, Paul Sammon says, is the *Blade Runner Director's Cut* on Warners Home Video (1993), VHS, Dolby stereo, Surround Sound, widescreen, 116 minutes, R-rated, with an aspect ratio of 2.41:1 (later released on DVD, of course). The film was re-invented yet again for an 'ultimate' DVD box set, with another 'director's cut' in 2007. This was dubbed 'the final cut', and contained further additions and revisions.

The 1992 *Director's Cut* came about when film archivist Michael Arick found a 70mm Workprint of *Blade Runner* in Warners' vaults; when Warners saw that this Workprint was doing good business when it was shown at special screenings,[70] with queues of Deckard lookalikes in long coats lining up around the block, they decided a *Director's Cut* release was possible.

Peter Gardiner began putting together an 'Enhanced Workprint', called *'Blade Runner:* The Final Director's Cut Version', in L.A., while Michael Arick was working on a different *Director's Cut* in London. There was a mix-up between London and L.A.; Warners wanted the *Blade Runner Director's Cut* to come out for a September, 1992 release, which they had organized. Consequently, Arick had to rush the job of putting together a *Director's Cut* for Warners, which he thought only approximated to Ridley Scott's ideas. The hospital scene, for example, didn't make it into the *Director's Cut*, partly because sound for the scene couldn't be found; additional violent footage didn't turn up; and there were various sound mistakes. (Arick had received a new set of instructions from Scott, when it was clear they couldn't complete the restoration in time – the new instructions included removing the narration, dropping the happy ending, and inserting the unicorn dream [FN, 365]).

69 Originally, Batty was going to kill Tyrell's family, a story point that Dustin Hoffman disagreed with when he was attached to the project. That scene was dropped, and subsequently stayed out of the film.

Oddly, 'father' was restored in the *Final Cut* of *Blade Runner*. Actually, 'father' has more philosophical and psychological resonance in the context than 'fucker'.

70 Such as at the NuArt: Hampton Fancher said he was amazed to see kids turning up in long overcoats and smoking Boyards cigarettes (FN, 340).

Director Ridley Scott was very intent on putting his beloved unicorn dream into whatever *Blade Runner Director's Cut* was going to be released; however, the shots he wanted were also lost; so a positive outtake was used for a new negative (which meant the unicorn shot was poorer quality than the rest of the picture, which makes it stand out – but in the wrong way).[71]

For Ridley Scott, it seemed the three main aspects of putting together a *Director's Cut* were losing the voiceover and the 'happy ending', and putting in the unicorn dream. One or two other additions were made: a woman's voice coming from the advertizing blimp says 'this announcement has been brought to you by the Shimata-Dominguez Corporation, helping America into the New World'; a new piece of Vangelis music is heard over the 12 second unicorn shot; and the violence in the International Cut was left out.[72]

Michael Arick also created a digitally remixed soundtrack for the film, and cleaned up and colour corrected it. The *Director's Cut* of *Blade Runner* is therefore not exactly what the director wanted, because footage and sound could not be found. 'The so-called Director's Cut isn't, really. But it's close. And at least I got my unicorn', Scott remarked (FN, 368).

❀

In 2007 the 'final cut' of *Blade Runner* was released. It followed the 1992 director's cut very closely, but included all sorts of additions, as well as altered elements (such as sound and dialogue). The additional elements to the 2007 cut included:

➤ dancers wearing hockey masks at Taffey's club;

➤ a new unicorn dream sequence;

➤ many new vistas of streets, buildings, panoramas;

➤ new or alternative close-ups;

➤ alternative or additional dialogue (no voiceover, though, of course);

---

71 The shot was an outtake that had been cast aside in favour of other footage of the unicorn, but it was the only piece of unicorn footage that could be found in the Rank vault in London.

72 Scott also wanted the shot of the giant eye put back in, and dialogue corrections (FN, 352).

➤ a new soundtrack including new dialogue, and new recordings of foley work.

✳

The unicorn dream sequence in the *Final Cut* was now more of a montage, intercutting between Deckard at the piano and different images of the unicorn. And Deckard is awake, not asleep (although the differences between waking dreaming, day dreaming, remembering, imagining, fantasizing and other states are hazy).

The *Final Cut* also contained new filming – Joanna Cassidy was shot on a greenscreen stage, so that her face could be superimposed on that of stunt performer Lee Pulford during her death scene (for some that would be an insult to Pulford, who died of cancer in 1997, aged 57). And Harrison Ford's son Ben was filmed, so his mouth could be replaced over his father's mouth in the scene where Deckard encounters Ben-Hassan (Ben Astar).[73]

The *Final Cut* was developed between 2000 and 2002, led by restoration producer Charles de Lauzirika (who worked on other Ridley Scott movies), and was then abandoned for some years (while the legal situation was ironed out). It was taken up again in 2006, and finally released in 2007. As well as the 'final cut' itself, a bunch of new documentaries were commissioned (headed up by *Dangerous Days*), and the workprint was also released (these additional materials came about largely because of the enormous expansion of the DVD market – now big movies had not one short 'making of' featurette, which might have been fed once upon a time to TV channels, plus a trailer or two, but in-depth documentaries on many aspects of the production, plus archival material, plus the critical response, and input from fans too).

The *Final Cut* was a restoration job in the digital age – the film was restored using all sorts of digital technology, including being scanned at a high resolution. As well as cleaning up the print, many elements were added or subtracted with digital tools: for instance, the cables that held up the spinners. OK, blurring out the shadow of a

73 But why not Harrison Ford himself? Well, you can guess why! Ford sure ain't gonna appear in any subsequent *Blade Runner* outings, sequels, etc.

camera operator or removing cables seems reasonable (but also can be seen as going too far – so there was a guy with a camera following the actor? So what? We *know* this is all fake!), but some of the additions and digital bits seemed too much (I think the teams involved in updating and reworking *Blade Runner* have missed the point about what a movie is, how movies work, why people watch movies, and why movies are valuable).

Other filmmakers, such as George Lucas and Steven Spielberg, have also gone back to some of their earlier films and restored them or altered them with digital technology. Spielberg and his team, for instance, inserted a computer generated alien into *E.T.* for the 20th anniversary release. And Lucas just can't leave any of his movies alone, going back over *THX-1138, Star Wars, The Empire Strikes Back, Return of the Jedi, The Phantom Menace*, etc.

For some, these re-issues and re-workings of existing movies are cynical and commercial, for others they are a chance to revisit pictures they enjoy. Hollywood is show *business*, and is *always* about money, but filmmakers such as Spielberg and Lucas don't *need* to drag earlier films from storage, dust 'em down, re-cut and rework 'em, and re-release 'em in theatres and on DVD. When you're worth $500 or $1 billion or whatever Lucas and Spielberg are worth, you certainly don't need to bother with goofing around with old celluloid from 1977 or 1982.

Thing is, if you keep revising and altering a movie, where does it end? A film is never 'finished', of course, but it does take up a place within people's memories. You shouldn't under-value how much viewers really like a movie, and they couldn't care less about so-called mistakes (it's the artists, of course, who see the flaws every time they look at their work. But that's a normal part of being an artist, you always see the mistakes first! And you always wanna go back and fix stuff).[74] The purist's line would be to leave it all alone, blemishes included. They are part of the charm of the

74 Besides, I don't regard continuity errors and the like as 'mistakes'. They are part of the movie. Movies are *stories* (even ultra-abstract, *avant garde*, experimental movies). It's all about *storytelling*, and things like occasionally being able to see some wires in a shot are incredibly *minor* elements in a movie-going experience. And the dweebs and nerds who point out editing or continuity flubs in movies really do need to get a life.

original film ('beloved mistakes'). If you start updating one part of an old movie for the digital age, you can keep going, updating every part. It gets silly (and very expensive).

Blade Runner is already very good – it's a masterpiece, for some fans. It doesn't need 'improving'. It doesn't need (or want) to be re-made. What would you do? Reproduce it shot for shot? The ultimate is colorizing classic movies. No, no, no.

THE UNICORN DREAM

The slow-motion shot of the unicorn running towards the camera stands out so dramatically from the rest of the film (no other character is given a dream sequence – but that's standard in movies – only heroes get the dream scenes or the back-stories). In the 'final cut' of *Blade Runner*, the unicorn dream is slightly different, and includes additional footage. However, like most symbols, the unicorn is ambiguous and can be interpreted in many ways. (It was meant to be mysterious, Ridley Scott said, that was partly the point, it was meant to be something Other in among the dark urban world of the rest of the film.75 It was also intended to be an image that only Deckard would dream about [FN, 276]). And it wasn't an implanted memory, of course – when did Deckard see a unicorn running through a forest?

The unicorn dream was shot using a white stallion in Black Park, near Pinewood Studios, in January, 1982; it was generally seen as Ridley Scott's own idea – Deeley, Peoples and Fancher all state it was Scott's concept (FN, 355). It wasn't a test, either, for Scott's follow-up film, *Legend*.

Other clues on Deckard's replicant status include the other blade runner (Holden) looking like him; both Tyrell's building and Deckard's apartment have Mayan designs; Deckard's eyes glow at one point, in the background of a shot, like the replicants' eyes do (there seems to be much

---

75 And it wasn't the unicorn that was important for Scott, so much as the green landscape surrounding it (FN, 377). A unicorn had appeared in Fancher's script, however, as part of a robot menagerie that Deckard kept.

more of that replicant glint in actors' eyes in the *Final Cut*).

Some of the hints that Deckard was a replicant were intentional,76 others were simply mistakes, due to the many script revisions. Hampton Fancher hated the idea of Deckard's eyes glowing, such an obvious way of telling the audience Deckard was a replicant; Harrison Ford also disliked the idea, as did Michael Deeley (ibid.). Fancher wanted the idea to be more ambivalent (FN, 362). For Slavoj Zizek, *Blade Runner*, via Deckard, presents a meeting between people and their own 'replicant-status' (1993).

I don't think the issue of Deckard being a replicant is that interesting, really, and it doesn't alter the film that much. After all, can't even replicants hope to find the girl of their dreams and run away from it all to hole up in the countryside?

Maybe audiences aren't that bothered about the Deckard/ replicant issue. Maybe they just see a guy doing his job, who doesn't like doing his job, who has to kill robots, which he doesn't like to do, who meets a woman he likes.

If Deckard *isn't* a replicant, then *Blade Runner* becomes very odd indeed, on one level: *it's a story about a man who falls in love with a robot, and runs away with her at the end!* That makes Deckard a strange guy, who can't get a girlfriend, so ends up going out with a machine. It's a guy and a sex doll, really, a guy and a love machine. And that's very creepy. 77 Creepy, but we know the lengths some guys will go to for sex!

But if Deckard *is* a replicant, then it's even stranger: the audience is watching (and loving) *a movie about two robots who run away together,* trying to find a little peace and quiet before their sell-by date destroys them. Either

76 David Peoples explained that the idea of Deckard being a replicant may have come out of the voiceover he wrote for Ridley Scott; or, rather, it was the way that Scott interpreted Peoples' metaphysical speculations about birth and God. Scott took up the notion that Deckard was a replicant and ran with it (FN, 361).

77 There're also odd notions – like, why would a secretary robot be fitted by the Tyrell Corporation with sexual responses and even genitals? Oh, maybe it was so bosses could enjoy their secretaries.

way, it's very odd.78

But then, maybe it's not bizarre at all: cinema history is full of creatures who have love affairs who aren't human: Disney's films, for instance, are stuffed with characters who are inanimate or animals or mythical beasts. It's no big deal to see lions making love in *The Lion King*, for example, or centaurs in *Fantasia*.

❀

Back to unicorns.

In Western mediæval symbolism, unicorns symbolized purity, innocence, virginity, and also Christ. Unicorns were shown, in mediæval paintings and tapestries, in flowery enclosed gardens with virginal women, and with the Virgin Mary. The unicorn might thus be linked with Rachel, a passive, idealistic, virginal type, a Virgin Mary to Deckard's Christ. The unicorn was a mythical animal, hunted down, an outsider, like Deckard; but it could also refer to Deckard hunting down the replicants, including Rachel (unicorns also have obvious phallic connotations).

One doesn't insert a pale, strange, symbolic shot into an otherwise dark and melancholy movie without considering the implications carefully; Ridley Scott, a painter conscious of his Celtic heritage (FN, 390), would have known something of unicorn symbolism (well, it's not particularly difficult to understand, like all symbolism – that's why it's a symbol!). Indeed, Scott later dived into Celtic and British mythology with William Hjortsbetg's fairy tale film *Legend*. But for Scott, the unicorn is also just an image, something intuitive, imaginative: if you have to ask 'but what does it mean?', you've missed the point!

Other critics have related the unicorn to Rachel, associating it with *The Glass Menagerie* by Tennessee Williams, which used unicorn motifs, where a character is described as 'different to other horses'. For some critics,79

78 Rutger Hauer thought it was sick: 'Deckard loving replicants didn't make any sense to me. Frankly, I thought Deckard was a little sick, because he ran away with a vibrator that *looked* like a woman'. The moral of the book, for Hauer, was that robots do not love you.

Ridley Scott, though, did not want to deal with the moral issues that the creation of the replicants raised. That would have made *Blade Runner* a different movie (in fact, it would be close to the 1972 *Solaris*).
79 S. Bukatman, 1997, 82.

having Deckard definitely a replicant (as the *Director's Cut* suggests) takes away the important ambiguity of the narrative.

SCRIPT CHANGES AND PLOT HOLES

Due perhaps to the many script revisions, many glitches appeared in the plot of *Blade Runner* (such as Pris and Batty knowing that Leon and Zhora had been killed, though they were holed up in J.F. Sebastian's apartment). The testing of the replicant, at the beginning of the film, is redundant, because the Tyrell Corporation would have comprehensive records of all the replicants it manufactured, and would easily be able to identify their own products (and later, when the police chief Bryant introduces Deckard to the replicants, there are full records).

Another weak point in *Blade Runner* is where Sebastian gets through Tyrell's security via the chess game; Tyrell has no security, no guards, no assistants (no Rachel), and not even a camera in the elevator (in this world of surveillance). Hampton Fancher had wanted Sebastian to deliver a small unicorn automata to Tyrell at his country estate, but budgetary restrictions had persuaded Scott and Deeley to go for the chess game (FN, 171). It has to be said that an elevator ride and a conversation about chess, which's what the scene amounts to, isn't the most exciting part of the film (though everyone is trying their best to build up the suspense. And, once again, Vangelis Papathanassiou's perfect score helps out enormously).

It's also not made clear why Rick Deckard has to hunt down the replicants, when they're going to die anyway (well, actually they are killing a lot of people as they travel back to Earth – a more formulaic or traditional film script would probably have opted to show the replicants being nasty villains at the start). If Deckard was such a good blade runner, he would have probably worked out that the replicants would try to get to Tyrell; it would be simply a case of guarding Tyrell and waiting for the replicants to arrive.

Another scene that was in an early draft of the *Blade Runner* script, but was never shot, was Batty and Sebastian going up another floor in the Tyrell pyramid, after Batty has killed Tyrell, to see the 'real' Tyrell, frozen in a cryogenic chamber because he had a terminal illness and was waiting for a cure (FN, 176), a common science fiction notion, entering the popular imagination in figures such as Walt Disney, who was thought to have been frozen after death (he wasn't, but the Walt Disney Company was).

There were originally six replicants; when Captain Bryant (M. Emmet Walsh) briefs Deckard on the replicants, he says there are six. The sixth was originally intended to be Mary (played by Stacey Nelkin),[80] 'an American dream mom', but her part was cut due to financial restrictions. In one draft, Mary was going to be seen on her deathbed, surrounded by the other replicants (Mary's scenes were dropped around the 3rd week of shooting).

Leaving out Mary caused some plot confusions, the most famous being: is Deckard a replicant?, a much discussed question. The unicorn dream is taken by many to prove that Deckard is a replicant; the unicorn is part of his dreams, which no one else could know about, so when Gaff leaves a tinfoil unicorn outside his apartment, it shows that Gaff knows of Deckard's inner thoughts, the implants the replicants have.

Some other elements that were dropped from *Blade Runner* included:

+ Rachel being morally superior to Deckard;
+ Hampton Fancher's ecological ending;
+ Deckard's dream of owning an electric sheep;
+ Zhora's snake dance, cut because of budgetary restrictions (although the stage set had been built – a pity because it would have made sense to cut to the snake performance after the shot of Deckard at the bar with the MC announcing the act heard off-screen);[81]

---

80 Nelkin had screentested for Pris. She was very disappointed when her part was cut. 'Stacey was devastated, poor thing. I still feel a bit badly about that', Scott admitted later (FN, 381).
81 It was another fight among the filmmakers – the director wanted to shoot the scene, but Tandem declined, because it would cost $200,000 (FN, 151).

+ Zhora being hit by a bus, after Deckard's shot her;

+ Leon hiding on a bathroom ceiling;

+ Pris having rats crawling over her, when she's at Sebastian's apartment;

+ Leon using a 'Black Hole Gun', which would emit a black beam;[82]

+ Deckard entering L.A. on a train;

+ three replicants escaping from a 'furnace asteroid';[83]

+ Deckard and Pris fighting in a gym;

+ two scenes of Deckard visiting the wounded Holden (Morgan Paull) in hospital, where Holden is recovering in a metal sarcophagus, not used, because Ridley Scott thought they weren't necessary.[84]

NARRATIVE STRUCTURE AND THE HAPPY ENDING

Blade Runner opens narratively in simple, A-B-C terms: like ten thousand other films (such as *Citizen Kane*, *Star Wars*, *Aguirre: Wrath of God*, and so on), it shows the setting of the film then moves in closer to introduce some of the lead characters. *Blade Runner* also employs the time-honoured narrative device of a journey, to lead in to the characters and story (here the spinner craft approaching the Tyrell Corporation building).[85]

In other respects, *Blade Runner* is constructed along simple narrative lines: the oppositions of the two men and two women, for example (Batty and Deckard, Pris and Rachel); the blond and the dark; the two couples; Deckard's fear and desire of both women, and so on. Also, despite being an influential science fiction thriller, *Blade Runner* contains a conventional Hollywood romantic plot, between

82 Invented by David Dryer, but, again, dropped for budgetary reasons, though a little hint of it remains (FN, 239).
83 These were sequences heavy on visual effects, which made them especially expensive, so they were dropped during pre-production. EEG said they couldn't deliver the shots required any cheaper (FN, 224).
84 These scenes crop up on the DVD of *The Final Cut*.
85 It isn't specified who is travelling to the Tyrell pyramid, or who the eye belongs to. It could be Holden, or Leon, or Tyrell, the Big Brother of the piece.

Deckard and Rachel. There are familiar exchanges between them ('do you love me?', 'do you trust me?'). And they are together at the end of the film, in both the 1982 version and the *Director's Cut* (and *The Final Cut*). The *Director's Cut* has the more ambiguous and 'darker' ending, with Deckard finding the paper unicorn and Gaff's voice heard in Deckard's thoughts 'too bad she won't live', and Rachel and Deckard moving into the elevator at his apartment block and the door shutting; however, the lovers are still together (and framed in the same cinematic space in a two-shot).

Many critics were disappointed with the ending of *Blade Runner*, the re-shot 'happy ending', apparently ordered by the studio.86 The pressures of traditional Hollywood narrative cannot be avoided, and the 'bad' couple, Batty and Pris, are eliminated, enabling Deckard and Rachel to ride off into the sunset, to fly away... where? Nowhere: they have no place to go, because the planet has been ruined (the helicopter shots for this part of *Blade Runner* were taken from 1980's *The Shining*; another connection with *The Shining* was the use of Joe Turkel as the head of the Tyrell Corporation: he had been the bartender in the Overlook Hotel; Hampton Fancher had wanted Sterling Hayden; and both movies were Warner Bros' productions).

Using Stanley Kubrick's *Shining* outtakes was Ivor Powell's idea; landscape footage had been shot in Monument Valley, led by Katy Haber, but it hadn't worked.87 So Powell called Kubrick up, and two hours later 17 2000-foot rolls of helicopter film were delivered (FN, 389). When Fancher saw the 'happy ending' he was 'beyond shocked', he 'could not fucking believe it... [it] was like waking up from a

86 The re-shoots lasted two weeks, in late March and early April, 1982. Inserts and additional photography also took place during post-production, into October, 1981, and January, 1982. Elstree and Pinewood Studios in London were the base for the re-shoots. The filmmakers had requested a number of re-shoots, including the snake dance, Deckard looking down from Sebastian's apartment roof, a new giant eye shot, a new elevator roof shot, a cityscape, a beefed-up intro for Batty on the computer screen in the police station scene, etc. Tandem nixed most of the re-shoot requests (FN, 278f). The bathroom scene was shot, though: here stunt co-ordinator Vic Armstrong, who had doubled for Harrison Ford in *Raiders of the Lost Ark*, stood in for Deckard searching Leon's bathroom. (The office scene was re-shot during principal photography).
87 Haber had filmed in Utah over 5 days with doubles of the actors, Deckard's car and a helicopter, in March, 1982, but the footage had been unusable. That was when Powell thought of contacting Kubrick (FN, 302-3).

nightmare – and then you didn't wake up!' (FN, 201).

Scott, Powell and a small crew shot the new ending with Ford and Young near Cedar Lake in California in late March, 1982.

But the happy ending was *planned* from early drafts of the script – it *wasn't* a case of the filmmakers being pressured into adding it after the sneak previews or due to the Ladd Company or Warners and production company Tandem. The filmmakers had run out of time and money to shoot the happy ending; and Ridley Scott had changed his mind about it, too, and preferred the tougher, ambiguous ending. But when the cards came from the previews in Denver and Dallas, the filmmakers decided that the happy ending might be a good idea to bolster the picture. So they were happy to shoot it.88 One of Hampton Fancher's earlier drafts had Rachel asking Deckard to kill her; another idea was to have Rachel go off and kill herself.

Terry Gilliam was so appalled by the ending of *Blade Runner* he was determined not to allow his film *Brazil* (1985) to be messed with (T. Gilliam, 146). But at least the rest of *Blade Runner* was good enough, and the scene didn't ruin the rest of the piece because it came at the end. When he saw the film at an Academy screening, with cast and crew in attendance, Fancher was very impressed:

> Man, when that first Vangelis music cue went *ka-BOOM!* and you saw that industrial landscape, people just sucked the breath out of that room. (FN, 319)

The happy ending isn't that big a deal, really. For a start, it's pretty short: there are big landscape helicopter shots and shots of Deckard and Rachel in the car, and some voiceover, and that's about it. The narration restates what Gaff has already said: who knows how long we'd have?

Anyhoo, this 'happy ending' ain't a 'happy ending': if you followed the dialogue in *Blade Runner*, you know the couple have a limited amount of time left. Plus, as fairy tales

---

88 One idea for the ending was to have Deckard's car driving through a forest into the desert. Another idea for the ending used the visual rhyme of the L.A. skyscrapers dissolving into the famous silhouettes of Monument Valley (FN, 301). Ridley Scott later employed Monument Valley in *Thelma and Louise.*

show, 'happy endings' of this kind (the holy couple of Western mythology re-united again), are not meant to be taken seriously. No one believes that everything's gonna be blissful just because the prince and princess get married (indeed, as some commentators have pointed out, that's the *start* of the problems!).

But the happy ending doesn't negate or let down the rest of the film that much, really. It's almost the sight of the lovely American landscape in full daylight more than the sentimentality of two lovers riding off into the sunset that jars, because the rest of *Blade Runner* is dark and rainy and always night and always urban. The sunlight and greenery and mountains is such a contrast with the rest of the picture, in feel and look, that it takes the viewer out of the previous 100 minutes, even more than the fact that the hero and heroine are riding off into the hills.

Because in both endings, of the director's cut and the US theatrical cut, the couple are together at the end of the film: both versions have a Hollywood 'happy ending'. Whether they walk into an elevator or into a car, the hero and heroine are *together* (and, in the *Director's Cut*, presumably they're gonna go from the elevator to Deckard's car and get out of the city – like the end of *Alphaville* (1965), another dystopian futuristic thriller).[89] What's way more disturbing is that our hero, whom the audience's been rooting for, is running away with a robot! And if he's a robot too, that's even weirder!

---

89 For once, in *Alphaville,* a Jean-Luc Godard film doesn't end with the heroes getting killed: Lemmy and Natacha manage to escape from Alphaville, driving away in a car at night. The movie closes with a – for Godard – very direct expression of love and tenderness: Natacha says the magic three words in a halting manner: 'je vous aime'. And she smiles. In close-up.

Who says Godard's cold and unfeeling? This is as soppy and gooey as the gooiest and sentimentalist Hollywood ending: the heroine saying 'I love you' as she drives away with the hero to a new life. It's cornball upon cliché upon gooiness in the extreme.

But it works.

The 1982 movie dropped Philip K. Dick's novel's reference to a post-nuclear world, though the *mise-en-scène* of *Blade Runner* is that of a post-atomic bomb world (but a lot flashier and slicker than, say, the *Mad Max* or *Terminator* films, made around the same time). Deckard was turned from a petty bureaucrat (the typical Dick hero) to a world-weary private detective.

Another aspect of Philip K. Dick's novel that *Blade Runner* didn't develop was the importance of animal life, which humans have nearly wiped out (hence the significance of Tyrell's owl, the stripper Zhora's snake, and the mythical animal, the unicorn). Deckard dreams of owning a real sheep (ironically, in the mid-1990s, one of the first animals to be cloned was a sheep called Dolly). Rachel's Voight-Kampff test included questions about spiders (according to Hampton Fancher, taken from one of Barbara Hershey's childhood dreams); Leon Kowalski (Brion James) was asked about a tortoise; rats infest Sebastian's apartment; Batty prowls and howls like a wolf and holds a dove; and Pris makes herself up like a raccoon (and rolls her eyes up, like a doll).

There was a short Animoid Row scene (on a $1 million set), as Deckard searches for the Egyptian manufacturer of Zhora's snake, and walks through a Middle Eastern-style *souk*, with different animals on show (a falcon, a donkey, an ostrich), accompanied by Vangelis's quasi-Arabic music.[90] The Animoid Row was a Cairo-style casbah, while Abdul Ben-Hassan was a stereotypical movie Egyptian, a Sydney Greenstreet type, fat, white suit, florid tie, in a fez (though with a futuristic optical device attached to his head).

It's a pity that the scene with 'the Egyptian', as he's called, is directed by numbers, without any flashes of inspiration. The visual design, though, is splendid, as everywhere in *Blade Runner.* Maybe it doesn't matter if the scene of a detective figure interrogating a guy in a store as he's on the

---

90 Vangelis has regularly incorporated musical styles from other cultures in his work – such as his album of Chinese-related themes, *China,* while his soundtrack for *1492* took on Spanish flavours (like his later album *Oceanic*), and for his brilliant score for *Alexander,* Vangelis took up Middle Eastern instrumentation and melodies.

trail of a mystery is so ploddingly done, because there's plenty of other stuff to be enjoying. A textbook example of how to really do those kind of common scenes in crime fiction is the work of Raymond Chandler (great as *Blade Runner* is, the detective elements ain't a patch on Chandler).

The Snake Pit sequence was suitably sleazy, with a crowded, smoky bar, people smoking opium with clay pipes, using long cigarette holders, drinking strange concoctions, and wearing high fashion. The Snake Pit was presided over by Hy Pyke's cynical sleazeball, Taffey Lewis. There's little build-up to Lewis, though, and his character makes little impression beyond being cynical and slimy. The scene concentrates more on Deckard's blurry state as he gets drunker.

MAKING *BLADE RUNNER*

Shooting on *Blade Runner* began on March 9, 1981, at Warners' Burbank Studios in Los Angeles (pre-production had lasted about a year – that helped to make *Blade Runner* a better film. The longer the pre-production period the better, usually. Or, to put it another way, had *Blade Runner* been rushed into production, it probably wouldn't be so rich).

The production of *Blade Runner* was fraught with problems, most of which are typical for many Hollywood movies: Harrison Ford and Ridley Scott fell out with each other, nearly fighting at one point;[91] Ford did not get on with Sean Young, and ignored her on set; that bothered Young, a lot. In an interview, she said she wouldn't dish any dirt, but acknowledged: 'I wouldn't call Harrison Ford generous' (FN, 214).[92]

---

91 Harrison Ford was fast becoming one of Hollywood's big stars at the time, appearing in two Star *Wars* films and *Raiders of the Lost Ark* immediately prior to *Blade Runner*. Ford remained an important Hollywood star, though he'd always tried to choose some 'serious' or prestige projects as well as the more routine Hollywood fare.

92 Sean Young was starting out in movies at the time of *Blade Runner*, and found it difficult to adjust to the multiple takes required of her. She said that the director shot 26 takes of her saying her introductory line in her first scene (FN, 214). Some in the crew dubbed the movie *Blood Runner*.

Harrison Ford was rough with Young during the love scene in *Blade Runner* (Michael Deeley called the 'kiss me, kiss me' scene 'the rape in the corridor', because it was so rough [FN, 164]);[93] the screenwriters disagreed with each other and with Scott; Philip K. Dick disagreed with Scott and his writers; the producers and Tandem didn't agree; the production company and studio disagreed about the film, and so on.

Harrison Ford was good casting for *Blade Runner*, which didn't require great acting chops, but more a certain look, attitude and style. Ford's short crewcut was one of the more memorable aspects of his performance. Apparently, the only other actor offered the role was Dustin Hoffman (other actors considered included Burt Reynolds, Nick Nolte, Al Pacino and Peter Falk). The filmmakers approached Hoffman partly because they needed a big star to keep the film afloat during pre-production. They worked with Hoffman in New York for a long time,[94] so Hoffman has also influenced *Blade Runner*, although he's not in it.[95]

Some in the team, such as Hampton Fancher, didn't like the idea of using Dustin Hoffman at all. (In fact, Fancher had been writing partly with Robert Mitchum in mind, the Mitchum of 1940s and 1950s *film noir* classics such as *Build My Gallows High*, a.k.a. *Out of the Past* and *The Night of the Hunter*, the remarkable, one-off, cult classic of 1955).

The filmmakers had been impressed with Harrison Ford when they visited London and saw the rushes of *Raiders of the Lost Ark*. Ridley Scott had liked the idea of using a hat in Deckard's look, which fitted in with the retro *film noir*

93 Hampton Fancher said the love scene was meant to be 'a very tender erotic moment. I was shocked and attracted by what turned up on the screen instead' (FN, 163). But Fancher hadn't wanted a sex scene at all in the film, and only wrote one reluctantly.

Apparently, there was more to the scene, too, with Rachel wrapping her legs around Deckard, and the lovemaking being less brutal (FN, 165). Parts of the unused footage appear on the DVDs of *Blade Runner*. Suffice to say, it's not one of the great love scenes or sex scenes in cinema history. Ridley Scott acknowledged that the scene was one of the least effective in *Blade Runner*.
94 Dustin Hoffman is well-known for contributing a lot to the movies he makes, with negotiations over the script which can run on for months. Hoffman is a movie star who will have all sorts of ideas about the character he plays.
95 Deeley recalled: 'we had wasted vital months trying to adjust the script to Dustin or vice versa' (2008, 214).

look he was going for. The notion was dropped[96] (but both Gaff and Bryant sport hats).

Casting on *Blade Runner* was by one of the most significant casting directors in the business – Mike Fenton (aided by Jane Feinberg and Marci Liroff). You can't over-emphasize the importance of casting on a movie, although, with films such as *Blade Runner*, there are many other components which overshadow it, like the visual fx, the sets, the look. Someone, for instance, had to cast all of the extras, who add so much to the street scenes in *Blade Runner*, and other people had to dress them and make them up.

Harrison Ford and Ridley Scott argued about the look of Deckard's character, as well as his personality. Scott wanted the grizzled, shabby look of Indiana Jones. Ford, meanwhile, didn't agree, and didn't want to play up the Humphrey Bogart/ Philip Marlowe connection either. 'I played a detective who did no detecting. There was nothing for me to do but stand around and give some vain attempt to give some focus to Ridley's sets', Ford remarked in 1991 (FN, 211).

Harrison Ford found Ridley Scott as unforthcoming about performances and acting as Sigourney Weaver had done in *Alien*. Ford said he'd look up to see Scott thirty feet up on a camera crane composing his shots, leaving him with little direction. He wanted to be directed. When filmmaker Alan Raymond visited the set he noted that Ford never said a word to Scott (FN, 210).

Crew members as well as the actors found Ridley Scott's perfectionism trying: shooting would be stopped while some prop or extra was moved an inch.[97] Scott also liked to direct looking through the camera, but the union stopped him doing that. Some in the crew found Scott a 'megalomaniac' and 'dominating'. The pressure of the arduous shoot resulted in some walk-outs (and there were Tee shirt gags, such as discontent over an interview Scott had done remarking that crews in Blighty called the director

---

96 Scott told Deeley, 'shit, I wanted that hat for Deckard!' Deeley replied that they'd lost a hat, but gained a star (M. Deeley, 215).
97 Art director David Snyder said that Scott wanted to change everything, that no set was shot just as it was built.

'guvnor': the Yanks responded with Tee shirts that read 'yes guvnor my ass'). It didn't help that the seven sprinklers employed to deliver the rain made shooting uncomfortable, plus the smoke, plus the night shoots. And Scott asking for take after take didn't help either.

David Peoples said sometimes he was writing scenes that would be shot the next day, and also 'just frantically trying to make certain changes to solve this particular thing or that particular thing'.98 Again, normal for a movie.

From day one the Warners production was behind schedule. As Alan Ladd recalled: 'after the first day of shooting the production manager called me to say we were now five days behind. Ridley had shot smoke all day'.99 Bud Yorkin and Jerry Perenchio at Tandem were impatient with the director's slow methods of working. As publicist Charles Lippincott put it, what Tandem saw coming from the set was 'rain, gloom, a woman being shot in the back, and a relentlessly perfectionist director who'd shoot the same sequence over and over again, all day long' (FN, 206). Maybe notions of replacing Scott were entertained, tho' everybody avoids replacing the director if at all possible.

The shoot was tense, as with *Alien*. Ridley Scott felt he was being questioned about every decision, which he was miffed about after making 2000 commercials and directing *The Duellists* and *Alien*. 'I was getting pissed off. Pissed off regularly. Every day', he recalled (T. Shone, 116). According to Katy Haber, the whole shoot was full of problems and tensions: 'it was just wretched awfulness, really; *Blade Runner* was a monument to stress' (FN, 202). Joanna Cassidy remembered that filming got 'brutal towards the end' (FN, 217) – particularly her death scene, which had to be achieved in one take, due to the pressure of time (i.e., money).

It's understandable that Warners and the producers would put pressure on the filmmakers, because this was a time when big films going over-budget and over-schedule

<hr />

98 T. Shone, 115.

99 There was also the first day on the Tyrell office set, where Scott wanted the columns turned upside-down. Larry Paull said, err, OK, come back at two p.m. The columns were duly up-ended. But the set had to be largely reconstructed later, as a matte painting by Matthew Yuricich.

were very much on their minds: *Blade Runner* was being shot not long after the very high budget productions of *Heaven's Gate, Raise the Titanic, Superman, Star Trek, Moonraker* and *Apocalypse Now*. The Hollywood studios weren't keen on letting film directors run away with productions. So a visual expert like Ridley Scott was at the time viewed suspiciously, even though *Alien* had been a big success. (Remember, though, that expensive movies such as *Superman, Star Trek* and *Moonraker* went on to make lots of money, but others didn't: *Raise the Titanic, Heaven's Gate* and *Honky Tonk Freeway,* for instance).[100] A movie like *Legend*, costing $30 million, which Scott directed 3 years later from William Hjortsberg's script, is a far, far greater disaster. (Incidentally, *Heaven's Gate* rivals *Blade Runner* for being shrouded in smoke, rain, fog and practical effects – it was a concern of United Artists about *Heaven's Gate* that you couldn't see what the hell was going on – for instance in the big battle at the end.)[101]

Philip K. Dick's response to the film was ambiguous and mixed; while impressed by what he saw,[102] there were many aspects he wasn't so keen on. He also didn't see the completed movie (or any of the subsequent adaptions of his fiction). Dick was asked to do a novelization of the film, but preferred to reissue his novel instead; he said he only made $12,500 from reprinting *Do Androids Dream of Electric Sheep*, but kept his integrity (FN, 282).

---

100 While *Heaven's Gate* lost plenty of money, there were other films of the time that lost plenty too, and films that were similarly expensive but were nowhere near as good as *Heaven's Gate*: *Honky Tonk Freeway* and *Raise the Titanic,* to name a couple. (*Honky Tonk Freeway* recouped only 2.1% of its $24 million budget).

101 *Heaven's Gate* was shot by one of the superstar cinematographers of the 'New Hollywood' era, Vilmos Zsigmond. He was DP on *Close Encounters of the Third Kind, McCabe and Mrs Miller, The Long Goodbye, Melinda and Melinda, The Deer Hunter, Heaven's Gate, Maverick* and *Deliverance* and would've been perfect for *Blade Runner.*

102 It wasn't exactly what he'd seen when he was writing the book, Phil Dick told the filmmakers, but the environment was very close, and he was dazed by the movie, according to David Dryer (FN, 284).

LOCATIONS

Ridley Scott spoke (in a Warner Bros. press release) of his technique of 'layering', filling the frame with 'a kaleido-scopic accumulation of detail', so that 'every incident, every sound, every movement, every colour, every set, prop or actor' was significant. For Scott, a film was 'like a seven hundred layer cake' (FN, 47). That attention to detail had really impressed Scott about *Star Wars*, and he was determined to put it on screen with *Blade Runner*. But it took a lot of effort and concentration, and some of the cast and crew felt they weren't getting the attention they wanted (FN, 387).

Certainly *Blade Runner* looks fabulous, with an amazing amount of detail in nearly every composition. *Blade Runner* was shot at Warners, in Burbank, on the backlot,[103] as well as several Los Angeles locations, such as Union Station and the Bradley Building, in downtown L.A., and the Second Street Tunnel.

The Old New York Street set (built in 1929) at Burbank Studios (now Warners) was dubbed 'Ridleyville' by the crew.[104] The Warners set was used for the Noodle Bar, the Animoid Row casbah, the nightclub and red light area, Chinatown, and the shopping arcade where Zhora (Joanna Cassidy) is gunned down. The set combined elements from Tokyo (the Ginza area), London (Piccadilly Circus), Hong Kong and New York (FN, 101). The streets were littered with wet newspapers and other junk; electronic 'Trafficators' controlled the movement of people (made mainly from parts of aeroplanes); shops were built out into the street; VidPhons; graffitied walls and booths; a newsstand displayed fictitious magazines (such as *Krotch*, showing a nude woman's torso on the cover, *Creative Evolution*, *Droid*, *Bash*, *Kill*, with a crazed dog on the cover, and a porn mag,

103 You can visit the Warner Studios in Burbank – highly recommended if you're a movie buff. You get to see the famous backlot and the New York sets.

104 David Snyder recalled he and Larry Paull and their team had 'bought every piece of pipe, plastic, steel and wood in a five-thousand mile radius' to get the street looking right (FN, 216).

It's actually quite a small backlot – compared, say, to the Universal backlot. Most of the backlots in L.A. are now shadows of what they used to be, of course, having been sold off for land.

Horn, featuring a scantily-clad woman on the cover, with cover-lines such as 'The Cosmic Orgasm', 'Scratch and Sniff Centerspread' and 'Hot Lust in Space').

After scouting locations such as London, Atlanta, Boston[105] and New York, the production team decided to film on the Warners' Burbank lot, where shooting could be controlled. Much of the film was made at night and in rain and smoke for the simple practical reason that it hid the limitations of the Burbank set (many a movie has followed the same procedure).[106] Ridley Scott didn't want *Blade Runner* to look as if it had been shot in a studio or a backlot, with the low hills not far away.[107] Smoke, rain and night shoots helped to push up the budget quite a bit, but they also added to the look and feel of the piece. And I don't think, ultimately, that audiences care that much whether a movie was made in a studio, a backlot, the script girl's cousin's aunt's daughter's bedroom or a plane circling the planet at 1,000 mph – they just want to enjoy a movie.

❀

Scriptwriter Hampton Fancher was wholly against using the Bradley Building in downtown L.A., at 304 South Broadway, because it's far too well-known, and had been seen on TV many times; he tried to persuade Ridley Scott not to use it. However, the production team transformed the Bradley Building into something new.

The exterior of Deckard's apartment was the 'Ennis-Brown house' at 2655 Glendower Avenue in L.A., a Frank Lloyd Wright building of 1924.[108] The apartment was intended to be one floor in a block of hundreds of storeys (Syd Mead designed the interior). It was meant to be claustrophobic, and cost $175,000, which Larry Paull said was way higher than any similar set he'd built before.

---

105 An abandoned housing estate in Boston was considered.
106 Seven sprinklers were mounted some 20 feet above the action for the rain.
107 The climactic battle on the rooftops was also shot on the backlot at Warners, on a movable 22 foot high set, though it was planned to film on existing buildings in L.A. (FN, 189). As Ridley Scott told Paul Sammon: 'I was really paranoid that audiences would notice we were shooting on a backlot' (FN, 379). Why, though? I don't think audiences care where a movie is filmed. They just want an entertaining coupla hours.
108 Used in numerous movies, including *The House On Haunted Hill*, *Rush Hour*, *Black Rain*, *The Karate Kid 3*, *Grand Canyon* and *Day of the Locust*.

The Second Street Tunnel was used for the approach to Deckard's apartment (you have to have a futuristic car going through a tunnel in a sci-fi movie). The Yukon Hotel was filmed inside the Pan Am Building, also in downtown L.A.

L.A.'s beautiful Union Station (at 8, North Alameda Street), built in 1939 in a Spanish Revival style (where you feel like you're in a movie), stood in for the police HQ;[109] a lengthy crane shot descends into Bryant's office, constructed in the huge Union Station interior (part of the set was left in the station, and is used today as offices).

The White Dragon Noodle Bar, seen at the beginning of the movie, designed by Lawrence Paull and Syd Mead, came from a hamburger chain called White Castle.

Hannibal Chew's Eye Works starred longtime character actor James Hong as the aged, obsessive genetic engineer, who talks sweetly to his beloved eyeballs in Chinese. He sports a heated fur coat with an array of pipes attached to it, and wears an optical headset. The Eye Works scene was shot over 2 days in Vernon, California, in a 7°-below food refrigerator.[110]

Tyrell's office was constructed on a Ken Adam *James Bond* scale, with a huge amount of space dwarfing the characters. There were 28 ft columns, 80 x 80 ft floor space, and a gigantic window looking out onto the Babylonian pyramids. Designer Lawrence Paull said Tyrell's office used a *moderne* look combined with an 'Establishment Gothic' or neofascist look. Ridley Scott and Jordan Cronenweth used Scott's customary 'future noir' illumination, with harsh side-lighting (plus unmotivated reflected light on the walls – as Doug Trumbull pointed out, there wasn't a reason for it, but it looked great). The re-dressed office set stood in for Tyrell's bedroom.

The overweening emphasis on surface and style in *Blade Runner* was exemplified in the Tyrell office scene

---

109 Union Station was also used in *Pearl Harbor, Charlie's Angels, Catch Me If You Can* and *The Replacement Killers*.

110 James Hong recalled that his scenes were shot 'under extreme pressure', trying to squeeze 5 days into two days: it was 'among the most tense I've ever worked in my life' (FN, 135). Michael Deeley said he had cut four days down to two for these scenes in order to make up some days in the schedule (2008, 232).

when Deckard says it's too light in the room: the windows are dimmed; not just a case of pulling the drapes, but a sequence with its own long shot and accompanying music to show the blinds sliding down the windows.

Sebastian's apartment was a strange, ghostly place, lit by Jordan Cronenweth with backlighting and sidelighting, in sepia, pink and white,[111] with whispers from the toys and automata added in post-production. Small actors and mime artists played Sebastian's toys. For Gothic strangeness and the authentic tingle down the back, *Blade Runner* was outdone by another film made at the same time: Ingmar Bergman's *Fanny and Alexander* (1982), which contained an unforgettable sequence set in the back of an antique shop, where the young boy, Alexander, wanders into a world of puppets that come alive.[112]

The filmmakers and fans often spoke of *Blade Runner* as an 'immersive' film, meaning, one supposes, that the look and feel of it encouraged immersion in the world of the movie. However, isn't all good cinema 'immersive'? Isn't all good art 'immersive'? It's another expression of fans of *Blade Runner* wanting to live in that world. A theme park ride or 3-D recreation of *Blade Runner* would certainly be popular among some punters. Geeks, Goths and gamers would line up around the block.

---

111 The reference here was to Mrs Havisham's Gothic house in Charles Dickens' classic *Great Expectations*, in particular the 1947 version by David Lean and Ronald Neame, one of the greatest British films. Hence Pris dressing in a veil.

112 *Fanny and Alexander* contains plentiful supplies of magic, fairy tales, ghosts and the supernatural. Fairy tales: *Bluebeard* (in the figure of the bishop and wife-murderer), *Hansel and Gretel* and *Babes in the Wood* (lost children). Magic: Ismael's talent for telepathy, hypnosis and killing the bishop; the statues and puppets that come alive (in the prologue, and in the antique shop). Ghosts: Alexander's father (and the bishop) coming back to haunt him, as in *Hamlet*; the bishop's two daughters.

The magic in *Fanny and Alexander* also relates to the perennial Bergman-esque theme of art and the artist: right from the beginning of *Fanny and Alexander* (in the prologue), Alexander is living partially in a magic world, when seemingly inanimate objects begin to move (such as one of the statues, of a white nude Venus, and a puppet of Death).

The visual effects in *Blade Runner* were not by Industrial Light and Magic, but they were very much in the ILM mould (ILM, though, would provide the effects for *Minority Report*). With *Star Wars*, Industrial Light and Magic established itself as the premier fx house in the world, a position it still holds today. ILM's fx developed a particular in-house look and style, which influenced pretty much every other effects house. In the late 1970s and through the 1980s, it consisted of smoky, backlit motion control shots of miniatures comped into the frame with an optical printer (Doug Trumbull had set the precedent, followed by so many fx houses, for that kind of hazy, glowing imagery in *Close Encounters, Star Trek* and *Blade Runner*). It was effects work of optical layering and superimpositions, bluescreen, rotoscoping, models shot with motion control, travelling mattes, stop and go motion, beam splitters and front projection.

The models were photographed in a dull, brown light, brown here connoting decay and death, a society in decline. It was the visual effects work, the superb matte paintings and miniatures, of the visual effects company EEG (Entertainment Effects Group), designed by Douglas Trumbull and Richard Yuricich, that added so much to *Blade Runner*.

The producers of *Blade Runner* clearly went for an expensive, impressive opening, with the extreme long shots of the L.A. wasteland evoking a kind of post-industrial sublime.[113] Note that the first shot of *Blade Runner* lasts for over 20 seconds: the producers wanted to milk the $2-3 million special effects sequence as much as possible.[114] It would be no good spending $3 million and having the shot on screen for only one second (the budget for 65 fx shots was c. $3.5 million. That's a tiny number of vfx shots by today's standards – but the visual effects here refers to the model and matte shots, and doesn't include the numerous

113 The long shots of L.A. include real landmarks, such as the cylindrical Bonaventura Hotel.
114 The Walkers scene in *The Empire Strikes Back* was, along with the Tyrell building approach in *Blade Runner*, cited more than any other visual effects sequence as the stand-out of the modern era.

shots with practical effects like smoke and rain).

The opening shot of L.A. was filmed on the 'Hades' set,[115] a table-top model 13 by 18 feet (designed by Tom Cranham), using Plexiglas sheets, foam and etched brass model buildings, lit by 2000 points of light and 7 miles of fibre optics. Photofloods shone up from underneath the set. The plumes of flame were optically added later, onto card on top of the chimneys, taken from explosions that Doug Trumbull shot for *Zabriskie Point* (1970), and from gasoline explosions filmed in EEG's car lot (EEG was then based at Marina Del Rey).

Doug Trumbull had been attracted by *Blade Runner*'s subject matter, of androids being indistinguishable from humans, and liked the setting of the film – in a run-down urban environment, instead of the usual outer space and clean spaceships of sci-fi movies. Trumbull remarked in 2007 that although *Blade Runner* is perceived as a visual effects movie, it has far less visual effects in it in terms of the number of shots – compared to, say, *Close Encounters* or *Star Wars*. But it was the way those shots were integrated into the narrative that made it seem as if they were far more.

Blade Runner benefitted a lot from *Close Encounters of the Third Kind*, because EEG now had all of the tools, cameras and working methods in place that had been developed on *Close Encounters* to be able to deliver the visual effects for *Blade Runner*.

EEG had developed its 'Icebox' motion control system for making multiple camera moves, and had used it on *Close Encounters of the Third Kind*. EEG employed a number of elements on *Blade Runner* that they had used on *Close Encounters*, including part of the mothership – seen in the circular roof of the police headquarters building.

The visual fx for *Close Encounters of the Third Kind* were shot on 65mm film, to minimize the grain and achieve a seamless integration with the live action 35mm footage.[116]

---

115 There were 3 stages at EEG used for *Blade Runner*: the big Hades stage and smoke room, Stage 2, where smaller models were shot, and Stage 3, where most of the smaller pieces, like clouds, video images and artwork were filmed (FN, 230).
116 *Close Encounters of the Third Kind* was shot in standard 35mm anamorphic.

The 35mm film was processed over a stop, explained DP Vilmos Zsigmond, so that it would match the grain of the 65mm film stock. Zsigmond said that one of the reasons the integration of fx, mattes, models and live action worked so well on *Close Encounters of the Third Kind* was because he and Trumbull helped each other out, and didn't fight.[117] That was important in *Blade Runner*, too.

For *Close Encounters*, the visual impact of the visually dense mothership was aided by Doug Trumbull's technique of shooting the model through smoke, diffusing the tiny lamps, creating areas of over-exposure on the large format film. Smoke was one of Trumbull's visual effects hallmarks, as well as Vilmos Zsigmond's.[118] A number of passes were shot of the UFOs, as usual on visual effects work – some for a halo or ring light effect, others for beams of light in smoke.

The motion control system for *Close Encounters of the Third Kind* used an early digital recording system, so that camera moves performed on the set in Alabama could be recorded and played back in the visual effects photography studio in Los Angeles. This enabled Doug Trumbull and the EEG team to shoot moving camera shots, instead of having the camera locked, as was usual up that point in movies involving optical or post-production effects. So the camera could follow Lacombe walking onto the apron, below the UFOs, and pan with him.

Like *Blade Runner* and *E.T. The Extraterrestrial*, *Close Encounters of the Third Kind* is largely a nocturnal movie, with key scenes occurring at night: Roy Neary first seeing the UFOs, Neary coming back with Ronnie, Barry going AWOL, the UFOs abducting Barry in in his garden, and the whole final section at Devil's Tower. Designed as masses of lights (like L.A. in *Blade Runner*), the UFOs are never shown in daylight. They always remain mysterious and awesome.

117 V. Zsigmond, in Schaefer, 1984, 321.

118 The mothership shots were achieved in a smoke-filled studio, sometimes taking hours to accomplish with the motion control camera crawling through a set-up. Dennis Muren, brought in to photograph the mothership, said some of the mothership shots would take a day and a half to perform, with the camera shooting a frame every few seconds. The smoke room was so dense with fog, moved around evenly by fans, sometimes the technicians couldn't see the camera when they went in every ten minutes to check everything was running OK.

Trumbull said:

> putting a UFO on the screen is like photographing God
> – people have a very abstract, mind's-eye view of what
> they expect to see in a flying saucer. So the general
> look we went for was one of motion, velocity, lumin-
> osity and brilliance. We used very sophisticated fibre
> optics and light-scanning techniques to modulate,
> control and colour light on film to create the appear-
> ance of shape when in fact no shape existed.119

In *Blade Runner,* the 3 foot model of the Tyrell
ziggurat, like the 6 foot skyscrapers, had to be well made,
because, as with Doug Trumbull's other deliberately slow-
paced special effects work, it would be on screen for a long
time.120 Trumbull spoke of wanting to create 'some crazy
illusion that looks so great that you can really hang on it like
a big master shot of an epic landscape' (FN, 79).

The computer-controlled camera technology, EEG's
Icebox, made multiple passes of the models, building up the
layers of detail. Using vaporized mineral oil to create smog
in the 'Smoke Room' enhanced the sense of aerial
perspective. The shot where Deckard goes out onto his
balcony was what Trumbull called an 'enhanced matte shot',
using a matte painting, live action, flying machines, and
movement on the street below (FN, 256).

One complex shot, called FX Shot 19 – of Deckard and
Gaff flying in the spinner over the city – contained 35
elements, included 20 miniature buildings, travelling mattes,
spotlights, strobes, 'RidleyVision' screens, Icebox camerawork, and different-sized flying models; the city view was
seen through the windscreen of the spinner: the shot also
contained the live actors and the many lights and screens
inside the spinner. Marrying the practical props with the vfx
was tricky, and some of the practical, on-set effects were
difficult to pull off: flying the full-scale spinner down a
street was a challenging shot, Terry Frazee said – orchest-
rating the prop on cables (on two cranes), the rain, the
lighting, and hiding the cables.

In some shots, 'geisha billboards' were added, as were

119 D. Trumbull in *Filmmakers' Newsletter*, 11, 2, 1977.
120 Only one pyramid model was constructed – and that only had two sides.

spotlights sweeping over the upper part of the frame (filmed in EEG's 'Smoke Room', then composited optically).[121] The 'blind' that Tyrell lowers was done by animation; the backgrounds and the upper half of the Tyrell room were matte paintings by Matthew Yuricich;[122] an fx shot of a spinner landing had to be dropped due to budgetary restrictions, so Ridley Scott and Jordan Cronenweth added one of their trademarks – rippling light reflected off water on the walls.

Doug Trumbull later moved into designing rides for theme parks; he founded Entertainment Design Workshop (one of his big early successes was the *Back to the Future* ride at Universal Studios. Other rides included IMAX ride-films for Universal Studios, and Circus Circus's Luxor Casino). Trumbull also had a go at directing, with 1983's *Brainstorm*. Not the greatest sci-fi film ever, but not a bad movie.

THE CITY OF THE FUTURE

The future Los Angeles of *Blade Runner* was a mix of Fritz Lang's *Metropolis*, New York's skyscrapers, and the neon-rich landscapes of Hong Kong, Tokyo and Chinatowns around the world, a postmodern collage of architectural styles quoting from other films, from postcards, advertizing, as well as real

121 These were shots with everything thrown in, including a kitchen sink – visual effects artists like to hide jokes in the back of scenes, so there's a kitchen sink in the back of one of the billboard skyscraper shots (similarly, there's a kitchen sink in the opening space battle in *Star Wars: Revenge of the Sith*). A model of the Millennium Falcon was stood on end to form a building in *Blade Runner,* as well as parts of the pyramid model.
122 Matthew Yuricich is one of Hollywood's great matte artists, working on *Close Encounters, Logan's Run, Star Wars, Star Trek* and *Forbidden Planet.* Yuricich replaced most of the set above the heads of the actors with a matte painting (FN, 253). The matte paintings in *Close Encounters of the Third Kind,* for instance, contributed so much to the movie. There are many matte paintings in *Close Encounters* – the distant views over the towns; all of the extensions to the Alabama indoor set; the long shots of Devil's Tower, and so on. And *Blade Runner* contains quite a few matte shots.

cities.[123]

Philip K. Dick's novel was set in San Francisco in 1992; *Blade Runner* was originally set in Manhattan (hence the constant rain); Ridley Scott wanted to feature the famous Chrysler Building in *Blade Runner*; Scott had used the title 'Gotham City' at one point; the modernism of New York City became the postmodernism of the City of Lost Angels. Los Angeles was chosen when so many locations in the city were used, such as the well-known Bradley Building.

Ridley Scott remarked that the city of *Blade Runner* could be seen as a combination of New York and Chicago, or of San Francisco and Los Angeles, a megalopolis of 100 million people. At one point the city was going to be called San Angeles, a giant city stretching between San Francisco and L.A. (that's a big city: they are 380 miles apart).

Ridley Scott admitted that his dystopian city in *Blade Runner* was 'overkill', but commented: 'I always get the impression of New York as being overkill' (FN, 75). Scott said the idea for the air traffic of the spinners came from his habit of landing by helicopter on top of the PanAm Building[124] in New York (the stylish way to arrive in Gotham City, the helicopter rides ceased when a helicopter crashed on top of the PanAm Building in the late 1970s).[125]

---

123 The *density* and *intricacy* of the futuristic city life evoked in the Japanese animated TV series *Cowboy Bebop* is just stupendous: it goes way, way beyond the city life portrayed in famous and celebrated city movies such as *Taxi Driver. Manhattan* and, yes, even *Blade Runner*, the god of future city movies for Japanese animators. Yep, even more accomplished and insightful than *Blade Runner*: because the city in *Blade Runner* was always stylized and fake like a ad-man's vision of the future (Ridley Scott claimed he had filmed about 2,000 commercials by the time he directed the Philip K. Dick adaption). It looked amazing, but it didn't have the depth of life and truth and *real people* that *Cowboy Bebop* has.

124 A PanAm building can be seen in the cityscapes in *Blade Runner*.

125 The accident may have inspired the famous scene in 1978's *Superman*.

SECONDARY CHARACTERS

William Sanderson's J.F. Sebastian was a prematurely aged 25 year-old, a loner and innocent, who made toys and dolls for rich clients, and to keep him company (the toys were mainly obtained from Benny Marvin, a toy collector in the San Fernando Valley). His character, being a misfit and ageing rapidly, mirrored that of the replicants.

Hampton Fancher created the idea of built-in obsolescence[126] from the earliest drafts of the *Blade Runner* script; it was a way of Tyrell sustaining his business (FN, 174). Sanderson had appeared in *The Coal Miner's Daughter, The Executioner's Song, Raggedy Man, Lonesome Dove* and *The Client.*

Gaff was played by Edward James Olmos as a fastidious, multi-lingual guy who sports extravagant clothes (bow-ties, fedoras, waistcoats, silk suits), blue eyes, an Italian punk hair-do, a French-Spanish mustache, yellowy Asian skin, and a walking stick. He was a Mexican-Japanese mix; he spoke a mixture of Hungarian, Japanese, Spanish, French, Chinese, German and English (Olmos created his version of Cityspeak himself, and brought a lot of work to a relatively small part. He has appeared in *Wolfen, Hill Street Blues, Miami Vice, American Family,* and *Battlestar Galactica*).

Gaff's origami constructions comment ironically on the narrative. The first one he makes is a chicken, referring perhaps to Deckard's refusal of taking on the blade runner job. Apart from the unicorn, another origami Gaff makes is of a man with an erection: 'the stickman meant Gaff thought Deckard had a hard-on because of the way he went after a case', said Olmos (FN, 129). It's certainly an odd idea – in a deleted scene, Leon enters his hotel room and looks at the origami figure in disbelief.

---

126 It was an old idea in manufacturing consumer goods.

Illustrations

✦ Some photos of locations used in *Blade Runner* I took in 2008.

✦ Some images from *Blade Runner*.

(© The Blade Runner Partnership/ Warner Brothers).

✦ Some influences on *Blade Runner*, such as *Star Wars*, *film noir*, and future cities.

(Courtesy of MGM; Universal; Columbia; Warner Brothers; Lucasfilm; and 20th Century Fox).

✦ Some images from *Total Recall*, *A Scanner Darkly*, *Next*, *Paycheck*, *Screamers*, *Impostor*, and *Minority Report.*

(Courtesy of Universal; 20th Century Fox; DreamWorks; Dimension Films; Lion's Gate; Carolco; Warner Brothers; Paramount; Miramax; Sony/ Columbia; and Columbia/ TriStar).

The art of Moebius (a.k.a. Jean Giraud), an influence on Blade Runner and many other movies.

Cities of the future: *Blade Runner* took inspiration from cities such as Los Angeles, New York City and San Francisco (above, photos by J.M. Robinson), and from Hong Kong and Tokyo (below).

Some reference points for Blade Runner: clockwise from top left: To Have and Have Not, Gilda, Metropolis, 2001: A Space Odyssey, Nighthawks, Star Wars, Touch of Evil and Heavy Metal.

Some of the movies based on the fiction of Philip K. Dick

TOM CRUISE

MINORITY REPORT

AVAILABLE ON DVD AND VHS

NICOLAS CAGE   JULIANNE MOORE

NEXT

AVAILABLE ON DVD SEPT. 25TH

ENTER THE SITE

WIDESCREEN COLLECTION

SPECIAL COLLECTOR'S EDITION

BEN AFFLECK   AARON ECKHART   UMA THURMAN

PAYCHECK

"A suspenseful thrill ride that will have you gripping your seat."
— Marisa Jerice, CBS-TV

(© 20th Century Fox, Carolco, DreamWorks, Dimension Films, Paramount, Columbia TriStar, Lion's Gate)

PETER WELLER   ROY DUPUIS   JENNIFER RUBIN

SCREAMERS

THE LAST SCREAM YOU HEAR WILL BE YOUR OWN

"AN APOCALYPTIC SCIENCE FICTION EPIC..."

— DIRECTOR'S CUT —

GARY SINISE   MADELEINE STOWE   VINCENT D'ONOFRIO   MEKHI PHIFER

From The Author Of Total Recall And Blade Runner!

IMPOSTOR

In The Future, Not Everyone Is Who They Seem To Be.

The Bradbury Building in downtown L.A.

Union Station in downtown L.A.

The New York set at Warners in Burbank, where much of *Blade Runner* was filmed (this page and the next page)

The French comic *Heavy Metal* (*Métal Hurlant*) and the artist Moebius (Jean Giraud, b. 1938) were among the visual influences on *Blade Runner*.[127] Mega-prolific Moebius designed Alejandro Jodorowsky's abandoned 1976 adaption of Frank Herbert's *Dune*, the animated *The Orphan From Perdide* (1982), the alien in *The Abyss* (1989), worked on *Tron* (1982), *Little Nemo* (1992), *Les Maîtres du Temps* (1982), *Willow* (1988), *Masters of the Universe* (1986), and designed the spacesuits for *Alien*.

Among Moebius's comic output were the *Jerry Cornelius* stories (from Michael Moorcock), *Arzach, The Long Tomorrow, The Horny Goof, Les Adventures de John Difool* (written by Alejandro Jodorowsky), *The Airtight Garage, The Onyx Overlord, The Fifth Essence* (later filmed by Columbia/ Gaumont/ Patrick Ledoux as *The Fifth Element*, 1997), *The Mysteries of the Incal, Is Man Good?, White Nightmare, Memory of the Future, Crystal Saga, Heavenly Venice, The Blind Citadel, Major's Holiday* and *The Goddess.*

Moebius was one of a few artists grappling with a 'concentrated city', a J.G. Ballardian 'metrocosm', the urban sprawl of Isaac Asimov, where a whole planet is a city (other comics dealing with the complex city included *Judge Dredd* and *Ranxerox*).

The metropolis was perhaps *the* site of cyberpunk fiction, urban conglomerates that swallowed up other cities (as in *Neuromancer* and *Blade Runner*), cities in crisis, urban dystopias. Phillippe Druillet and British artist Angus McKie also published in *Heavy Metal*, and created hi-tech visions of scale and monumentalism, enormous spaceships dwarfing cities.

Métal Hurlant was launched in 1975 by Bernard Farkas, Jean-Pierre Dionnet, Jean Giraud and Philippe Druillet. It published mainly French fantasy illustration, and spawned versions and translations in other territories, including a US version, *Heavy Metal*, in 1977. There was also an animated film, *Heavy Metal* (1981), based on the characters and art

127 Ridley Scott was a big fan of Moebius and *Heavy Metal*, and remarked that *Blade Runner* was an attempt at turning a comicbook into a movie.

from the magazine. Fantasy and comicbooks are still hugely popular in France.

Artist Syd Mead was a key influence on the look of *Blade Runner*, and the most prominent artist attached to the project (Mead had previously worked on the first *Star Trek* movie).[128] Mead was responsible for the design of many elements, including the flying spinners.

Other influences on *Blade Runner* included William Hogarth's engravings, Jan Vermeer's lighting (a favourite with filmmakers), Jacob Riis's photos of New York City, and Edward Hopper's paintings (in particular *Nighthawks*). Hopper's clear, dream-like, hypnotic images of urban life have a 'cinematic' quality, and can be transferred onto the cinema screen.[129] Hopper's silent, empty paintings have influenced other films (such as *Dick Tracy*, Warren Beatty, 1990). 'I was constantly waving a reproduction of [*Nighthawks*] under the noses of the production team to illustrate the look and mood I was after in *Blade Runner*', Ridley Scott said.

U GOT THE LOOK

Like so much self-conscious cinema, of the European New Wave onwards, *Blade Runner* is full of images of eyes, screens and looking:[130]

▸▸ the extreme close-up of the 👁 in the opening sequence[131] • the owl's eyes in Tyrell's HQ • the eyes grown in the genetic engineer's laboratory, Eye Works (sheep's eyes

128 Mead's going rate at the time was $1,500 per day. (That's still good money!)

129 The photograph in the Esper scene consciously evoked Vermeer and Hopper (FN, 258).

130 Science fiction cinema is full of screens and technological ways of seeing, as Garrett Stewart pointed out: sci-fi cinema is filled with 'banks of monitors, outsized video intercoms, x-ray display panels, hologram tubes, backlit photoscopes, aerial scanners, telescopic mirrors, illuminated computer consoles, overhead projectors, slide screens, radar scopes, whole curved walls of transmitted imagery, the retinal registers of unseen electronic eyes'. (In E. Rabkin, 1985).

131 A number of films have a close-up of an eye in their opening sequences: *White of the Eye*, *The Eyes of Laura Mars*, *Black Widow*, *Dream Lover*, *Incubus*, *Repulsion*, *Vertigo* and *Blade Runner*.

and plastic replicas were used) • Tyrell's eyes behind their thick spectacles (gouged later by Batty on a model of Joe Turkel's head) • Pris's eyes opening with a click on the Voigt-Kampff machine (stock footage from Oxford Scientific was used) • the eyes blown-up in the Voigt-Kampff test (with the replicant's eyes glowing red, like the owl's)[132] • Deckard and Rachel talking to each other via video telephones.

The giant �s emphasizes the paranoia of being watched: it's a conscious allusion to Big Brother in George Orwell's *1984*. There are many screens in *Blade Runner:* of the giant billboards and neon signs on buildings (in the Leon-Deckard fight scene, a woman on one of the billboards was going to be seen reacting to the fight in a wide master shot) • the 'RidleyVision' screens advertizing the Off-World colonies • the screens of the Voigt-Kampff and Esper machines • several computer screens • screens on the Trafficators • screens on the VidPhons • and the many photos. The 'Oriental' video commercials were shot at EEG; the women were filmed taking pills, or smoking, or flirting with the viewer.

The way *Blade Runner* is photographed also emphasizes the gaze: many of the shots use long lenses, creating close-up images carved out of the detritus of the world (long focal lengths being one of the hallmarks of the smoke and back-light school of cinematography popularized by the TV-commercial-turned-film directors of the Seventies onwards).

The Esper machine sequence plays with looking and lying: it reworks a favourite movie with filmmakers and cultural theorists, *Blow-Up* (Michelangelo Antonioni, 1966),. Deckard controls the virtual examination of Leon's photograph with voice commands like a movie director, the computer zooms in on parts of the photo, blowing them up with extraordinary detail, making them 3-D, as technically unbelievable in *Blade Runner* as enlarging the photo in

---

132 The Voigt-Kampff machine was 'a stroke of collective genius', Ridley Scott said: first Phil Dick had come up with a 'totally believable instrumentality and term', which Hampton Fancher 'brilliantly expanded and deepened', and finally Syd Mead had come up with 'a marvellous design for a working model of this imaginary thing. All of these accomplishments were quite extraordinary' (FN, 382).

Blow-Up.[133]

The Esper sequence makes cultural critics go gooey – it's all about looking, dissecting, analyzing, reframing. It's pure cinema (and it's very much an *editor's* scene, it's about montage as much as about looking: consider the way the scene is put together with a series of reaction shots of Deckard and reverse angles of Deckard at the machine, as well as frame grabs from the machine itself.[134]

There are further lies to the Esper machine sequence: in the studio set, there was Rutger Hauer and a stand-in, and a stand-in for Zhora. As Hauer said, the Esper sequence

> shows how you can play with images and tell a story and, at the same time, completely bullshit someone. Which is just like making a motion picture, come to think of it. (FN, 146)

Using stand-ins has been part of movie-making since its beginnings in the late 19th century, though – not just for stunts or nude scenes, but in numerous other ways.[135]

For Scott Bukatman, a terrific commentator on vfx and cinema, the Esper scene 'with its fantasied control of the projected image, is a most hypnotic meditation on cinematic power' (1997, 47), and 'the most hypnotic demonstration of cinematic suture and control in contemporary cinema' (1993, 136). As Hampton Fancher and David Peoples recalled on their wonderful audio commentary for *Blade Runner,* it took a lot of narrative work to set up and get to the Esper scene (but it was worth it). It came about partly because of Harrison Ford's complaints that he didn't do much detecting.

---

133 Garrett Stewart, one of the best critics on the philosophy of photography and looking, says the Esper sequence is a lyrical exploration of reality and illusion: 'think of it this way: the photo is, in short, cinematized – edited, cut, motorized, even lent the illusion of three-dimensionality resulting from shifts of perspective as the camera roams the already fixed image plane.' (1999, 11)

There was originally going to be much more of the Esper supercomputer – it was going to appear on the streets, and inside cars (FN, 120).
134 *Blade Runner* is quoted in a lengthy sequence in *Ghost In the Shell: Stand Alone Complex* (2002) which uses the famous Esper scene in the 1982 Warners movie. Cop Togusa takes some photos and explores them like Deckard in *Blade Runner.*
135 The Esper scene was partly re-shot, in London, by Filmfex and Lodge/ Cheesman.

Birds are another motif: Tyrell's owl; the eagle by Tyrell's bed; the herons behind the bed on a screen; the owl on Tyrell's robe; statues of birds in Tyrell's office. Daryl Hannah was sometimes shot at slower speeds, to give her movements a quick, jerky quality, like a bird's, a technique used for her death scene (FN, 180).

Like other British film directors who spent years in advertizing (Hugh Hudson, Alan Parker, Adrian Lyne), Ridley Scott and Jordan Cronenweth employed complex lighting, much backlighting, tracking shots, and long lenses. Cronenweth and Scott seemed to have decided that nearly every shot in *Blade Runner* could be backlit, in keeping with the future noir look, often with spotlights. There was also a surprising amount of handheld camera, offering a looser feel to the otherwise highly stylized and formally precise film.

Two focal lengths were favoured in *Blade Runner*'s visuals: wide angle shots, with elaborate, painterly, deep focus compositions, and long lenses. After using one or two wide angle shots to establish a scene, the filmmakers filmed much of *Blade Runner* using very long lenses, following people around apartments or along streets zoomed-in, in close-up, creating a claustrophic feel. One never knows exactly how, for example, Deckard's apartment is furnished – there is never an establishing shot depicting the whole main room, showing where the couch or piano is. Instead, Jordan Cronenweth covers the scenes in Deckard's apartment using either medium close-ups with a long lens, or low angle medium shots. Further, Deckard's apartment is dimly lit, with spotlights flashing into the windows regularly, like a lighthouse beam. (You simply have to accept all that unmotivated light, which moves through the scenes in *Blade Runner*: those spotlights outside Deckard's window, for example, are clearly only a few feet away from his windows, but he's meant to be on the 97th floor. Where do they come from? It doesn't matter – it looks cool. The mobile spotlights were Jordan Cronenweth's idea).

Rain and smoke suffused *Blade Runner* – smoke from cigarettes, from the streets, from the spinners, from the haze over L.A. As in Forties *film noirs*, many of the characters in *Blade Runner* smoke (opium in the Snake Pit, but usually French Boyard cigarettes). The spiralling smoke was inevitably picked out by stylized backlighting; cinematographer's Jordan Cronenweth's favourite shot was of Rachel smoking in Tyrell's office during the Voigt-Kampff test.

There was a great emphasis on costumes and fashion, and intricately decorated sets. Ridley Scott wanted *Blade Runner*'s world to look lived-in, everyday, shabby, it was not a 'hardware' film. *Blade Runner* was a triumph of art direction and lighting design, with post-punk fashion prominent (in the look of Pris and Batty especially).[136] 'In *Blade Runner* I would go so far to say that the design is the statement', confessed Scott.[137]

The costumes (by Michael Kaplan and Charles Knode, with hair by Shirley Padgett and make-up by Marvin Westmore and Bridget O'Neill), combined high fashion, post-punk chic, Asian contemporary, and plenty of retro, 1940s, *film noir* look. The costumes both describe the characters and the world, but also pop out of the screen. The number of extras wearing goggles, for instance, is unusual, yet also fits in with the highly polluted environment the film is trying to evoke.

The hero would've sported a hat, to go with his updated trenchcoat, but that was one of the few stipulations that Harrison Ford had about his character: *no hat*, because he'd worn one for months on *Raiders of the Lost Ark*. But the trenchcoat, his one suit, and the shirts and ties all placed Deckard within a 1940s æsthetic (though updated to the early 1980s).

Rachel was given the *femme fatale* treatment, icy, cool, immaculate, with fitted suits, tons of lip gloss and bright red lipstick,[138] and very flamboyant coats. Pris was decked out in a post-punk girlie outfit, with a micro skirt, stockings, a yellow zebra-stripe jacket, bleached blonde wig,

136 Daryl Hannah said she got the idea for Pris's heavily made-up eyes from Klaus Kinski in the wonderful film *Nosterfatu* (1979). The blonde fright wig Hannah had found when she was preparing for her screen test. Hannah was 21 at the time of filming, and had appeared in *Paper Dolls*, *The Fury* and *Hard Country*. Pris's look crops up in *manga* – in *Akira* and *Dominion: Tank Police*, for instance.

137 R. Scott, *Cinefantasique*, 12, 5-6, 1982.

138 The Eighties was the decade of lip gloss, of course. Young remembered that Scott wanted *lots* of lip gloss on Rachel.

and dark make-up around the eyes. She might have been the lead singer in a post-punk rock band, one of those Goth outfits playing industrial, doom-laden music such as the Cure, Bauhaus or the Cult.139

Roy Batty was given a high collar, updated version of the classic black leather jacket, one of the stereotypical outfits of rebellious youth ever since movies like *The Wild One* (1954), with Marlon Brando (Batty's the lead guitarist in *Blade Runner*'s post-punk band). The cropped, bleached hair placed him as a twin to Pris (they are the post-punk couple, contrasting with the retro, Forties look of the dark-haired couple, Deckard and Rachel). In some variants, Batty also sported face paint, and a map tattooed on his chest (which can be glimpsed only fleetingly). Undoubtedly the oddest wardrobe choice for Batty was having him strip down to tight cycling shorts.

Blade Runner's streets were inhabited by a mixture of ethnic groups and types: chanting Hare Krishnas, punks in spiky hair and shades, Chinese in large hats riding bicycles, people carrying umbrellas with fluorescent tubes, German, chain-wielding midgets sporting goggles (they might have wandered in from a Werner Herzog movie),140 cops with neo-fascistic uniforms and body armour, and so on. The filmmakers wanted a host of Asian extras to populate the streets: they were given coolie hats (made from baskets). The idea was to have everyone looking different – to reproduce the variety of a real city.

The headgear alone in *Blade Runner* is very odd – like the umbrellas, it's to provide protection against the acid rain. And the masks, too, to combat pollution (but you can see all those sorts of things in cities like L.A. today).

There were sushi and noodle bars; traffic signals (Trafficators) that robotically intoned 'don't walk' or 'move on' and were festooned with video screens; parking meters which threatened to kill law-breakers; giant Babylonian, Roman and Greek-style pillars; Chinese dragon neon signs; sleek cars beside overcrowded 'Megatrans' buses; and over-

139 It was Michael Kaplan's idea to have a scene of Pris applying her raccoon make-up.
140 In particular, Werner Herzog's bizarre early movie *Even Dwarfs Started Small* (1971).

head, the spinners of the LAPD, the blimps advertising Off-World vacations (with phrases such as 'Breathe Easy', 'All New' and 'Best Future'),[141] giant 'RidleyVision' video billboards, forests of neon signs, the ever-present acid rain, and the towering skyscrapers and apartments. As Paul Sammon wrote,

> it is to this bewitching visual surface which most viewers repeatedly return. Like its industrial counterparts in the worlds of high fashion and architecture, *Blade Runner* is a form of ultra-sophisticated "designer cinema", one whose astonishingly complex visual field has, despite a subsequent decade's worth of futuristic/ alternate world spectaculars like Tim Burton's *Batman* trilogy or the recent *Judge Dredd*, remained the high-water mark against which all other big-budget SF entertainments are measured. (FN, 3)

Blade Runner is a film in love with lights and lighting: from the opening sequence onwards, with its panorama of L.A. at dusk, with the plumes of fire and the thousands of lights of the city, *Blade Runner* bristles with lights. As with Douglas Trumbull's other visual effects work (on *Star Trek* and *Close Encounters*, for example), the models in *Blade Runner* contain thousands of tiny lamps (the Tyrell pyramid in particular houses many lights).

Throughout *Blade Runner* lamps dominate the *mise-en-scène*: they shine through the windows of Deckard's apartment (with its *film noir* blinds, also culled from Bernardo Bertolucci's *The Conformist*, a film that influenced directors like Francis Coppola, Paul Schrader and Martin Scorsese);[142] nightclub spotlights swirl above Sebastian's Bradley apartment block; the blimp advertizing Off-World

141 EEG produced 15 TV commercials, directed by David Dryer, to be used in the film (FN, 241). Later movies, such as *Minority Report*, would develop the commercial angle even further.

142 *The Conformist* was a key film for the 'New Hollywood' generation. Filmmakers such as Francis Coppola, Paul Schrader, Joel Schumacher, Sydney Pollack and Martin Scorsese cited it as an influence. Cinematographers such as John Bailey and Michael Chapman admired Vittorio Storaro's work on that film immensely. Bailey (DP on *American Gigolo, Ordinary People, Cat People* and *The Big Chill*, among others) said (in 1984) that he'd seen *The Conformist* probably 25 times. For director Adrian Lyne, *The Conformist* 'is probably the best single film ever made. It's the perfect blend of visual and performance' (in J. Gallagher, 1989, 167).

vacations (a 4 foot model) is a Christmas tree of lights; the flying spinners have prominent headlamps, with disco lights on their roofs; their interiors are a forest of lamps.

Cinematographer Jordan Cronenweth said the lights were meant to be like prison search lights, invading people's privacy (H. Lightman, 1982). The lights also make noises – the ones outside Deckard's apartment make a whooshing sound as they rotate, like a lighthouse.[143] Ridley Scott said the shafts of light derived partly from the Thatcher Library and screening room in *Citizen Kane*.[144] There's no particular justification for the lights that shine into Deckard's apartment, like UFOs from *CE3K*, apart from the simple fact that they look good (there were explanations offered, such as the air traffic flying by). You'd think Deckard would get pissed off with 'em, and close the blinds (but drapes and curtains are never closed in movies, for practical as well as narrative and æsthetic reasons). Some of the influence for the huge amount of lamps on-screen and the OTT lighting fx likely comes from *Close Encounters of the Third Kind*: look at the extraordinary sequence where the UFOs buzz the Guilers' home and take away little Barry. I can't think of a movie before *CE3K* which has lighting and smoke used like that.

Blade Runner is founded on strong vertical and horizontal lines: the verticality of the skyscrapers, elevators, and shafts of light from above; the horizontality of the streets, the apartments, the window blinds, and the shafts of light entering the buildings.

Deckard's apartment is conceived as a cluttered, low-ceilinged space, often shot from a low, knee-high viewpoint, emphasizing the claustrophia (the most famous example of low ceilings as psychological oppression occurs in *Citizen Kane*). The design of the Tyrell Corporation building drew on Egyptian pyramids and Mayan and Aztec ziggurats; creating an atmosphere of wealth, power and grandeur, a 'op

---

143 Many of the wonderful sounds in *Blade Runner* were created by Jim Shields.
144 *Citizen Kane* was a favourite movie of Ridley Scott's, as with so many filmmakers, and his company, Scott Free, produced a TV movie about the making of Orson Welles' masterpiece, *RKO 281* (1999). It's not surprising, then, just how much *Citizen Kane* looms behind *Blade Runner*.

Egyptian extravaganza'.[145] The allusion to ziggurats and temples also evoked gods and sacrifice.

There is much on-screen advertizing in *Blade Runner*: logos for Coca-Cola, Atari, Budweiser, Trident, Michelob, Jovan, Shakey's, Jim Beam, and TDK are shown, for example. Sometimes the product placement is very prominent: in the climactic sequence, where Batty sits down and dies, he is framed against a giant TDK sign. Designer Lawrence Paull said the neon signs were not given to the film by the companies, but the companies paid for them to be made (by neon specialists American Neon). Some of the neons came from Francis Ford Coppola's expensive Las Vegas musical *One From the Heart* (1982), which probably uses more neon than any other movie. DP Jordan Cronenweth aimed to shoot by the available light coming from the neons.

VANGELIS

Vangelis Papathanassiou's music for *Blade Runner* contributed so much to its mood and impact. With the visuals so stylized and busy, it was a wise choice to have the music held back and simple. It was his music for *Blade Runner* and *Chariots of Fire* that made Vangelis's name, at least in the film world (although a single, 'Albedo 0.39', had attracted attention in 1976, and with Jon Anderson Vangelis produced the memorable 'State of Independence').[146] Undoubtedly, it's *Chariots of Fire* that has been quoted or spoofed in popular culture more than any of Vangelis's other works (*Bruce Almighty, Madagascar, How the Grinch Stole Christmas, National Lampoon's Vacation, The Real Hustle, Late Night With Jimmy Fallon,* etc).

Vangelis Papathanassiou (born March 29, 1943, in Volos, Greece) made his base in London and Paris for much of his career (his Nemo Studio was in central London, near Marble Arch). His most well-known early incarnation was in the band Aphrodite's Child, with singer Demis Roussos (who

145 G. Bruno, in A. Kuhn, 1990, 187.
146 'State of Independence' has also been quoted in pop culture, and was given an all-star treatment by Donna Summer.

can be heard warbling on the *Blade Runner* soundtrack).

Other soundtracks Vangelis produced included *The Bounty* (1984), *Mask* (1985), *Nosferatu a Venezia* (1987), *Francesco* (1989), the S/M fantasy *Bitter Moon* (Roman Polanski, 1992), *Missing* (Costa-Gavras), *1492: Conquest of Paradise* (Ridley Scott, 1992), and the ancient world epic *Alexander* (Oliver Stone, 2004). Vangelis also provided the title music for epic *Cosmos* TV series (Carl Sagan), and for Frederic Roussif's French films *Opera Sauvage* and *Apocalypse des Animaux*.

Vangelis Papathanassiou's solo efforts tended to be 'concept albums', in the prog rock manner, taking on notions such as 'Antartica', 'China', space travel ('Albedo 0.39'), or the painter El Greco. Essentially a studio recording artist, Vangelis tended to be reclusive, rarely performing live, giving interviews, or playing the PR game. For many years he lived in London, working out of his home studio, Nemo.

Due to contractual problems, and perhaps due to Vangelis himself (there were rumours that he had too much to do, or wasn't so keen on the music towards the end, or was reluctant to finish it), an 'official' soundtrack album of *Blade Runner* was delayed, and several bootlegs came out, even before the movie was released. The 'official' soundtrack was released on Atlantic in 1994, and included excerpts from the dialogue in the film. (Vangelis took longer to deliver the music than the producers hoped: he was contracted in December, 1981, and delivered the score in April, 1982. Vangelis is a composer who likes to do everything himself, and for a big movie soundtrack, that can take months instead of the usual weeks). In 2007, a 25th anniversary edition of the soundtrack was released, which contained some deletions from the movie, and also some (not so distinctive) music inspired by the film (plus more, somewhat distracting voices).

As well the soundtracks noted above, Vangelis's albums included *The Dragon* and *Hypothesis* (both 1971), *Earth* (1974), *Heaven and Hell* (1976), *Albedo 0.39* (1976), *Spiral* (1977), *Beauborg* and *China* (both 1978), *Short Stories* and *See You Later* (1980), *Private Collection* (1983), *Soil Activities* (1984), *Rhapsodies* (1985), *Opera Sauvage* (1987),

Direct (1988), *City* (1989), *Page of Life* (1991), *Voices* (1996), *El Greco* (1998) and 'best ofs': *Best of Jon and Vangelis* (1984), *Themes* (1989) and *Portraits* (1996).

Vangelis Papathanassiou's solo and soundtrack music was marked by low drones, washes of string synthesizers, the patter of drum machines, chimes and bells, slow or half-time rhythms, echoey Moog and Arp siren calls, and simple musical patterns (sometimes two chords, sometimes one throughout, often major chords). Vocals were rare (instead, Vangelis used samples, or swathes of mellotron and choral samples).

Vangelis's music was about texture and atmosphere, rather than melodic or structural ingenuity, or *virtuoso* technique. It was dark, moody music, which took itself seriously, and tended towards the bombastic and operatic.

Vangelis was shown *Blade Runner* in an unfinished state, but was very impressed by it – 'thrilled' and 'terrified', he said. Vangelis is known for being cautious about accepting assignments to score a movie. Oliver Stone said he had to go back to Athens four times before Vangelis agreed to score *Alexander* (2004).

For *Blade Runner*, Vangelis used his customary washes of string synthesizers, tinkling pianos, and hi-pitched *glissandos*. For Sebastian's toy-filled apartment, Vangelis employed soft sounds;[147] for the threatening scenes of Batty and Leon, the prerequisite bassy synth drone was used; sad saxophones accompanied images of the lonely replicants and blade runners; for Deckard's dream, Vangelis used a plaintive piano;[148] the sound of echoey children's laughter is heard when Deckard contemplates Rachel's photograph of herself with her mother (which becomes animated, with the

[147] Andrew Hoy recalled that around this time Vangelis was fascinated by percussion, and mixing percussion instruments with synthesizers. 'Gongs and bells lay everywhere,' Hoy said, 'Vangelis used to collect them like a magpie' (FN, 273).

[148] There are a couple of moments where Vangelis's score merges with the diegetic sound of Deckard and also Rachel playing the piano, a nice musical moment. For Mary Ann Doane, the scene with the photographs condenses a number of critical terms, including 'representation', 'the woman', 'the artificial', 'the technological', 'history' and 'memory'.

The temp music which editors William Zabala and Terry Rawlings had put with the scene was by Maurice Ravel (his *Piano Concerto*). Vangelis, however, used one of Chopin's *Nocturnes* instead (FN, 162).

shadows moving);[149] Vangelis used one of Frédéric Chopin's lyrical *Nocturnes* (the 13th) as a basis for Rachel's piano music; towards the end, to accompany Batty, a synth sounding like a cat wailing was employed. Generally, Vangelis's music was held-back and wistfully melancholy, permeating the dark, weary, downbeat atmosphere of the film.

Other music in *Blade Runner* included Gail Laughton's New Age *Harps of the Ancient Temples*, jazz, and the plangent Japanese *biwa* and voice folk song played by the floating blimp. British light music singer Peter Skellern also appears, as well as the portly Greek vocalist Demis Roussos (both odd choices for a futuristic Hollywood thriller!).

For Pauline Kael, Vangelis's music was overwhelming, which 'gives the picture so much *film noir* overload that he fights Scott's imagery; he chomps on it, stomps on it, and drowns it' (1986, 362).

BLADE RUNNER AND THE SUBLIME

Blade Runner is one of a number of science fiction films which emphasized the sublime: *2001: A Space Odyssey* is the obvious case, but also the pictures of Steven Spielberg (*Close Encounters of the Third Kind, Jurassic Park, A.I., E.T.*), *Star Trek, Solaris, Avatar* and *The Abyss.*

For a useful guide to the sublime in cinema, art critic Christopher Hussey defined seven aspects of the sublime (in art, relating to the Romantic era), derived from critic Edmund Burke: obscurity (physical and intellectual); power; privations (such as darkness, solitude, silence); vastness (vertical or horizontal); infinity; succession; and uniformity (the last two suggest limitless progression).[150]

These tenets of the sublime in art can be applied to cinema – to films such as *Blade Runner, Citizen Kane* and *Apocalypse Now*, movies which consciously encourage notions such as obscurity, darkness, vastness and infinity.

---

149 The photograph was a freeze frame of some extras shot on the Burbank backlot; the shot shifted from a freeze frame to a regular running speed.
150 C. Hussey: *The Picturesque*, Putnam's, New York, 1927.

Ridley Scott and Philip K. Dick disagreed about the nature of the replicants, so central to *Blade Runner*. For Dick they were 'deplorable', 'cruel', 'cold', 'heartless', and 'less-than-human'. They represent people who've forgotten how to be human, how to empathize: they are like Nazis. But Scott saw them as supermen who were 'smarter, stronger and had faster reflexes than humans'. Scott considered Dick's notion of the replicants as intellectual, and said he wasn't interested 'in making an esoteric film' (FN, 285).

The replicants are slaves, and work in the 'Off-World colonies', recalling the slave trade of Western nations. Another view is that *Blade Runner* portrays a conservative, reactionary politics (in keeping with the early 1980s Reagan era): Deckard's white alienated male is seen struggling in a multi-racial ghetto, confronting a variety of ethnic types (Egyptian, Chinese, Japanese). In that view, Deckard is in the minority, the white man surrounded by immigrants and other cultures.

For some critics, the replicants are at the centre of *Blade Runner*'s exploration of reality and dream, the imagined past and the real past, real and implanted memories. The replicants are an expression of a certain strand of postmodern theory, as espoused by Jean Baudrillard, who spoke of postmodernism as the era of simulcra and simulation. The replicants are pure simulcra, human doubles, down to their forged memory implants. These themes of reality/ fiction, real/ imaginary, are reflected in the tensions between the modernist and postmodern look of the movie, its 'retrofitting', the evocation of the future using elements of the past (director Ridley Scott said *Blade Runner* was 'a film set 40 years hence, made in the style of 40 years ago' [Warners press release]).

In this view, *Blade Runner* is a postmodern hybrid, using the past – 1940s *film noir* styles – to recreate the future. For Scott Bukatman, *Blade Runner*'s vision of the city is perhaps really modernist, 'a more deeply-historicised restatement of fundamental modernist ideas of the city' (1997, 60). Some of the 'retrofitting' is obvious – Rachel's hair and costume, for example, recalling the *femme fatales* of *film noir*, such as Lauren Bacall or Joan Crawford. Ridley Scott referred to Rita Hayworth, in the 1946 film *Gilda*, in connection with Rachel, though Sean Young sure ain't Rita Hayworth ('Rachel was my homage to *Gilda*, in a way' [FN, 383]). So Deckard's cop is a 2019 version of the Humphrey Bogart private detective, out of the stories of Raymond Chandler and Dashiel Hammett.

ROY BATTY AND THE REBEL ANGELS

> Fiery the Angels rose, & as they rose deep thunder roll'd
> Around their shores: indignant burning with the fires of Orc
>
> William Blake, 'America'

In the climactic fight, Roy Batty acts up a strange, playful and camp mixture of child and ruthless hunter; he strips down to cycling shorts,[151] howls like a wolf, lopes along around the interior like an animal, paints his face, pouts, returns to Pris's bloody body, and taunts Deckard in a British accent about fighting in a 'sporting' manner, about Deckard being man enough to fight. He also comes across as a Christ crucified and the god Pan.

Rutger Hauer said it was largely his idea that Batty should act like he was involved in a silly, wicked game ('more playful and strange than simply witnessing the last swan song of a machine', said Hauer [FN, 186]). Pauline Kael saw Hauer's performance as ridiculous, 'a shoo-in for this year's Klaus Kinski Scenery-Chewing Award', bringing

> the wrong kind of intensity to the role – an effete, self-aware irony so overscaled it's Wagnerian. His gaga performance is an unconscious burlesque that apparently passes for great acting with the director. (1986, 363-4)

---

151 Tom Shone called Rutger Hauer's replicant 'Nietzsche in cycling shorts'.

Certainly, when one watches Rutger Hauer throughout the picture, he is very camp; for instance, look at the scene where he enters J.F. Sebastian's apartment and gasps 'what great toys you have!', then as the shot progresses, between cuts to and from Daryl Hannah's punkette Pris, Hauer gives one of his Little Boy Hurt expressions as he talks about Leon's death. This childish frown also occurs just at the end of the celebrated shot of Hauer in the elevator, after murdering Tyrell.

Batty becomes superhuman, smashing his head through a bathroom wall, punching his hand through a wall, able to sense where Deckard is through walls and floors, able to lift up Deckard with one arm, and so on (Hauer thought the sticking-his-head-through-the-wall scene was over-the-top. It wouldn't be in a Chinese martial arts movie).

At one time in the script's genesis, Batty was to be dressed 'somewhere between a Comanche warrior and a transvestite' (S. Bukatman, 1997, 84). This section of *Blade Runner* takes on the narcissistic display of the male body found in many action films (consider Sylvester Stallone, Mel Gibson, Bruce Willis and Arnold Schwarzenegger, who often strip off).

♣

Roy Batty in *Blade Runner* quotes William Blake and is portrayed as a Blakean rebel angel, a fallen Lucifer-type (he is depicted as a fallen angel after killing his creator, Tyrell, in the elevator outside the Tyrell ziggurat, when he looks up, shivers and the stars are seen for the only time in the film ['the expression of Rutger's face is so – well, I've never see anything like it on film before', commented Hampton Fancher [FN, 178]). The stars were shot with the track-zoom effect used in *Vertigo* (Alfred Hitchcock, 1958).

Tyrell calls Batty the prodigal son. In the climactic fight scene, Deckard and Batty are identified with each other (both are wounded in the hand, for example); there are also homoerotic overtones in this scene. The identification is complete when Roy rescues Rick, in a gesture of redemption and sacrifice (director Ridley Scott also said that Batty was being 'more human than human' here, more humane than Deckard, who wants to kill him, and he also wants someone to watch him die.)

Roy Batty introduces himself with lines from William Blake's poem 'America', a pæan to the American Revolution and the founding of modern America. David Peoples had put in a quote from Percy Bysshe Shelley's 'Ozymandias' in the scene where Batty kills Tyrell, and Ridley Scott suggested putting in some Blake too.

Batty's death soliloquy was cod lyrical, in keeping with the camp/ sinister way Hauer played the character:

> 'I've seen things you people wouldn't believe. Attack ships on fire off the shoulder of Orion. I watched c-beams glitter in the dark near the Tannhauser Gate. All those moments will be lost in time. Like tears in rain. Time to die.'

David Peoples, not Rutger Hauer, as some claim, wrote the speech (FN, 195-6). Batty's character, like the others in *Blade Runner*, can be seen as a manifestation of the decline of modern America (Deckard and Tyrell are obvious examples of moral and social decay). The opening shots of *Blade Runner* depict Los Angeles as a 21st century Gomorrah or Hell, all pollution, decadence and darkness, with the fires of Hell raging intermittently from giant chimneys.

For writer Hampton Fancher, Batty saves Deckard's life partly because he appreciates Deckard's 'last, defiant, life-affirming gesture', as Deckard 'literally spits in the face of death' (FN, 194). For Thomas Byers, Batty's gesture is heavily ironic, one killer saving another, an act which questions Deckard's masculine identity. As Batty stalks Deckard he torments him with questions, such as 'aren't you the good man?'; after Batty's death, Gaff tells Deckard 'you've done a man's job'. Deckard's not sure whether he's as 'good' a man as Batty, or even if he's a 'real man' at all.[152] Ridley Scott thought maybe Batty wanted Deckard to witness his death, so he could tell others what had happened, and why the replicants should be treated like humans (FN, 193). Fancher said he never envisaged Deckard getting the better of Batty: it was always Batty who would win the fight.

---

152 T. Byers, "Commodity Futures", in A. Kuhn, 1990, 44.

Blade Runner questions human identity – this is a film in which the robots or cyborgs are more 'human' than the humans themselves. For critics such as Hal Foster, Mark Dery, Claudia Springer and Scott Bukatman, cyborgs in contemporary cinema are 'a last bastion of overdetermined human, masculinist definition, bodies armoured against the malleability and invisibility of the present' (S. Bukatman, 1993, 17).

Batty also recalls Christ, impaling his hand with a nail (in order, presumably, to prolong his life); the white dove, another Christian symbol, flutters up to a suddenly blue sky when Batty dies; however, Batty is not wholly a Christ-figure, having just murdered his 'father' and maker, Tyrell. In postmodern fashion, the Christian symbols and motifs are evoked but shorn of their power (the white dove and blue sky come out nowhere, narratively illogical, the imagery more reminiscent of a pop video).[153]

Although Batty is the Blakean 'dark angel', and Deckard the saviour, it is Batty who is associated with light, while Deckard is clad in dark clothes. However, Batty's blond appearance in his black leather jacket recall a different kind of Superman, Friedrich Nietzsche's *Übermensch*, mistakenly taken up by the Nazis. The replicants, via Batty and Leon, evoke Adolf Hitler's vision of an Aryan Master Race (recall the replicants' strength, blondness, racial 'purity' or pure origins, as machines). As 'positive monsters', then, the replic-ants ambiguously recall fascism (Ridley Scott conceived the replicants as 'supermen').

The blond man in his black leather jacket is also a gay image; Nazis have often been portrayed as homosexual or sexually 'perverse' in Hollywood films. Batty, though, is given heterosexual aspects – exchanging furtive looks with Pris, and kissing her (a 'kinky' moment, by conventional standards, occurs when Batty kisses the dead Pris, pushing

---

153 Hauer said the dove was his idea, and he hoped it wouldn't be only interpreted along Christian lines, because 'there's a lot of interesting connections to birds in mythologies and religions other than Christianity' (FN, 192-3). The dove was a last minute idea, and Scott wasn't sure if it would work – 'it's a bit on the nose, don't you think?' he told Hauer. Scott admitted that the bird he filmed next to the incinerator at Elstreee Studios didn't quite fit in (FN, 384).

her tongue into her mouth).[154] But when Batty kisses Tyrell before killing him, it was not meant to be seen as homosexual or sexual, said Rutger Hauer; it wasn't a 'kiss of death', either, but just a farewell.

The shadow of Thirties Germany is also conjured up in the sleazy downtown bar, the Snake Pit (shot on the redressed Sebastian's apartment set), where Zhora works as a snake dancer: the camp (off-screen) voice of the master of ceremonies announcing the acts ('watch her take the pleasure from the serpent that once corrupted man') recalls Joel Grey in *Cabaret*, and also Peter Sellers mad scientist in *Dr Strangelove*. Another view (Kaja Silverman, 1991) is that, as a slave leader, Batty's 'hyperbolic whiteness' is a kind of blackness, which separates the issues of race and slavery.

TIME, MEMORY, REALITY

Blade Runner's David Dryer (visual fx) said there was a lot of *Metropolis* in *Blade Runner* (FN, 111). Aside from *Metropolis*, *The Big Sleep* and *The Maltese Falcon*, *Blade Runner* also alludes to *Blow Up*, in the Esper photographic sequence, where Deckard scans one of the replicant's photos.

Blade Runner is thus part of a trend in Hollywood movies to raid the past, and particularly the history of cinema, then mix the elements together. Simultaneously *hommage* and parody, in which old films are used more than real history to recreate the future. In this respect, *Blade Runner* is a nostalgic film, lovingly evoking the history of cinema, exploring the viewer's nostalgia for cinema, the memory of Forties *film noir* (*Blade Runner* was shot on the Warners' lot where *The Maltese Falcon* and *The Big Sleep* had been filmed).

---

154 That was Hauer's idea, Daryl Hannah said (FN, 183).

PHILIP K. DICK'S FICTION AND POSTMODERNISM

It's become a multiple cliché layered upon countless clichés in contemporary criticism to call *Blade Runner* and Philip K. Dick's fiction 'postmodern'. But they are. The argument is over on this one, but consider the following opposites:

modern	postmodern
industrial	post-industrial
reality	post-reality/ simulation
feminism	post-feminism
epistemology	ontology
depth	surface
centre	boundaries
inside	outside
subject	object
transcendence	immanence
time	space
order	flux / flow
mind	artificial intelligence
communities	networks
hermeneutics/ semiotics	acts/ performativity
body	machine/ cyborg
biology	biomechanics
sex/ reproduction	genetics/ replication

It's also commonplace to discuss *Blade Runner* and Phil Dick's cinema in terms of (yawn) cyberspace and cyberpunk (*Blade Runner* is lumped together regularly with movies such as *Tron, The Terminator, Aliens,* and other 1980s movies). What does cyberspace and cyberpunk mean? Well, cyberspace is a technological mirror, a place of infinite (digital) desire, reflecting back the virtual narcissism of the subject (Ovid by way of Julia Kristeva). The internet here is the ultimate inner space, which only individual imaginations can traverse, not groups, organizations, or institutions. A pleroma of connections always leading back to the self. E.M. Forster's 'Only connect', but connecting only with self. (The dream of total transparency, the fusion of self and techno-logy, is a paradoxical one, because the technology is always there, always makes its presence felt. There is a desire to *become* the technology, but also to keep it always at a distance.)

This is all very much central to Philip K. Dick's speculative fiction, and to all of the films based on his stories. The ambiguity that Dick's fiction feels towards technology (and its manifestation in global consumerism) is fundamental.

> We are living in a system of technological temporality [asserts Paul Virilio], in which duration and material support have been supplanted as criteria by individual retinal and auditory instants...

It's a world in which the question of modernity and postmodernism has been replaced by *'reality* and *post-reality'* (1991a, 84). It's not Baudrillardian 'simulation', Virilio suggests, but 'substitution': 'new technologies are substituting a virtual reality for an actual reality' (1994b).

Cyberspace is also a 'nonspace' (*Neuromancer*, 63), a constructed space, and thus predictable, and therefore easier to understand than physical space.155 It's noteworthy that the internet uses spatial metaphors: cyberspace, infoscape, chat rooms, surfing, navigation (*cp.* Arjun Appardurai's concept of 'scapes').156 An electronic cartography, a geography of gigabytes.

Scott Bukatman (one of the best writers on *Blade Runner*) coined the phrase 'terminal space' to cover everything from virtual reality, interactive systems, computer games and flight simulators, to special effects movies, computer art and digital graphics on TV (1993, 107). What was true in 1993 (the year of Bukatman's key book *Terminal Identity*), is even more so now, with a 'cyberspace look' or 'cyber-style' occurring across many technological platforms: the internet, computer software, lifestyle magazines, fashion, TV ads, MTV and pop promos, CD cover design,

155 J. Bolter: *Turing's Man: Western Culture in the Computer Age*, University of North Carolina Press, Chapel Hill, 1984.
156 A. Appadurai: "Global Ethnoscapes", in R. Fox, ed. *Recapturing Anthropology*, SAR Press, 1996.

children's TV, sci-fi in movies and TV, and so on.[157] For Bukatman, William Gibson's infoscape is a graphic but limited metaphor for the global economy, a theme park reduction of the circulation and organization of capital.[158]

Cyberspace is also the space of finance, capital and ATMs ('cyberspace is where your money is'). In cyberspace, crimes are difficult to detect: money can disappear into offshore accounts at the touch of a button.[159] And it's the realm of information and espionage war, being fought with computers, spy satellites and electronic espionage. And in cyberspace, replicants are virtually indistinguishable from humans (your identity in cyberspace can be virtually any-thing, as sci-fi movies such as *Ghost In the Shell* have demonstrated poetically).

CYBORGS AND CYBERCULTURE

Cyborgs, robots and human 'hybrids'[160] have been a standard component of science fiction since the first great classic book of sci-fi and horror, Mary Shelley's *Franken-stein*. Since then, popular culture has been awash with cyborgs, androids and robots: the robot Maria in *Metropolis*, Gort in *The Day the Earth Stood Still*, *Forbidden Planet's* Robbie, *2001's* HAL, R2D2 and C3PO, the 'droids in *Star Wars* (partly based on the peasants in Akira Kurosawa's *The*

---

157 By the early 2000s, delivery systems were converging: interactive television, the internet, broadcasting, mobile phones, PCs, ISDNs, digital subscriber lines (DSL), satellites, wireless application protocol (WAP), broadband, and so on.
158 S. Bukatman, in L. Cooke, 1995.
159 Organised crime generates $750 billion a year, with drugs making $400-500bn, according to Z. Sardar (Z. Sardar & J. Ravetz, eds. *Cyberfutures*, Pluto, 1996). See also: "The Wired Scared Shitlist", *Wired*, 3, 1, Jan, 1995.
160 On cyborgs, cyberspace and cyberpunk, see: S. Bukatman, 1993; D. Haraway, 1985 and 1989; J. Prosser, *Second Skins: The Body Narratives of Transsexuality*, Columbia University Press, N.Y., 1998; E. Rabkin, 1987; S. Brewster, 2000; T. de Lauretis, *Technologies of Gender*, Macmillan, 1987; J. Rusher, 1995; B. Rux, 1997; P. Schelde, 1993; F. Botting, 1999; J. Telotte, 1996, in N. Ruddick, 1992, and "The Tremulous Public Body", *Journal of Popular Film & Television*, 19, 1, 1991; J. Bergstrom: "Androids and Androgyny", *Camera Obscura*, 15, 1986; R. Barringer, 1997; A. Balsamo, 1988; C. Berg, 1989; C. Springer, 1993; D. Larson: "Machine and Messiah", *Genders*, 18, 1993; G. Schwab, 1987; P. Warrick, 1980; C. Fuchs, 1993; F. Glass, 1989.

Hidden Fortress [1958]), Lee Majors in *The Six Million Dollar Man*, Yul Brynner in *Westworld*, Arnold Schwarzenegger in the *Terminator* series, Judge Dredd, RoboCop, Tetsuo in *Akira*, Ash in *Alien*, Number Five in *Short Circuit*, the Mark 13 cyborg in *Hardware*, *Max Headroom*, Data and the Borg in *Star Trek*, the military cyborgs in *Universal Soldier*, Max in *Dark Angel*, Haley Joel Osment's David in *A.I.*, television sci-fi (*Dr Who*, *Stargate SG-1*, *Farscape*, *Babylon 5*, *Blake's 7*, *Futurama*, *Total Recall 2070*, *The Bionic Woman*, *Quantum Leap*), plus 1,000s of robots and cyborgs in *animé* and *manga* (*Cyborg 009*, *Neon Genesis Evangelion*, *Gundam*, *Macross*, *Appleseed*, *Dominion: Tank Police*, *Black Magic*, *Bubblegum Crisis*, *Mazinger Z*, *Gunbuster*, etc), and so on, not to mention children's toys (such as War Planet, Transformers, Digimon, Beast Wars, Warhammer), and the thousands of characters in comic books, cartoons, TV series, films and computer games which are turned into merchandising: *Teenage Mutant Ninja Turtles*, *The Mighty Morphin Power Rangers*, *Pokémon*, *The Mask*, *Tank Girl*, *X-Men*, *Men in Black* and *Judge Dredd*. And of course in Philip K. Dick's fiction: the replicants in *Blade Runner*, Arny's Quaid in *Total Recall*, etc.

For some commentators (David Bell, 2000), the cyborg is not limited to the characters in *The Terminator* or *Star Trek*, but texts can be cyborgian, or founded on a cyborgian consciousness (transgressing Cartesian epistemologies and Western philosophy's dualisms). They reaffirm bourgeois, dominant ideology, conventional notions of good/ evil, male/ female, human/ machine, self/ other (A. Balsamo, 1999).

Of course, contemporary Hollywood cinema doesn't get much further than the sensational image of humans interacting with cyborgs at the most extreme levels: sex, violence and death. Even movies enshrined by the critical academy, such as *Blade Runner*, don't go much beyond the titillating question: 'what's it like to fuck an android?'

The hospital scenes, featuring Deckard and Holden, which were dropped from *Blade Runner*, contain some absolutely vital information on this matter: Holden asks Deckard if he fucked the snake woman before killing her.

The dialogue's in that locker room, macho fashion (*Blade Runner*'s a very macho movie), but it's a key point, about having sex with the androids. Holden tells Deckard (in the deleted scenes on the DVD releases) that Deckard shouldn't have a crisis of conscience about it – it's like fucking your washing machine, then switching it off (sex followed by death). Deckard doesn't really respond to Holden's taunts: if this scene comes *after* Deckard has made love with Rachel, the scene has a new dramatic inflection. The filmmakers left the scenes out, as they don't seem to add much to the film, but the exchange about having sex with Zhora is absolutely central to the theme of *Blade Runner*, not only the romantic sub-plot.

Associated with the cyborg or robot are the many monsters in the horror genre, what Slavoj Zizek calls 'return of the living dead': Leatherface in *The Texas Chainsaw Massacre* (with his trademark mask and chainsaw extension). Anti-heroes with knives for fingers (Freddy Krueger in *A Nightmare On Elm Street* and the youth in *Edward Scissorhands*). 'Jaws' in the *James Bond* films of the 1970s, with rows of metal teeth. *Hellraiser*'s Pinhead. Ghosts (*The Sixth Sense, What Lies Beneath, The Others*). Demons and the Devil (*The Exorcist, The Devil's Advocate, Spawn, Angel Heart*). Vampires (*Dracula, Buffy, Van Helsing, The Lost Boys, Interview With the Vampire*). Sub-humans or mutants (*The Fly, Basket Case*). Zombies (George Romero's movies). Werewolves (*An American Werewolf in London, Wolf, The Howling*). Devilish aliens (*Gremlins, Critters, Independence Day*, the *Alien* series). Poltergeists (*Poltergeist*). Killer dolls (*Magic, Child's Play*). Witches (*Salem's Lot, The Craft*, the *Blair Witch* films). And psychopaths and serial killers (the *Friday the 13th, Candyman, Scream* and *Hallowe'en* movies).

For critic Donna Haraway, the cyborg represents the possibility of new identities, moving beyond binaries, boundaries, universalisations. Transgression is a key theme in Haraway's thinking. New sutures, new borders. For Haraway, the technological revolution is as significant as industrial capitalism (1985). In "A Manifesto For Cyborgs", Haraway offered a chart of transitions 'from the comfortable old hierarchical dominations to the scary new networks I have called the informatics of domination'.

Here, simulation replaces representation, biotics replaces organisms, surface replaces depth, obsolescence replaces decadence, replication replaces reproduction, genetic engineering replaces sex, robotics replaces work, 'fields of difference' replaces the nature / culture binary, and 'cyborg citizens' replaces the public and private (we are all cyborgs claimed Donna Haraway; Haraway has famously proclaimed herself a cyborg, a quintessential technological body [1985]).

In Harawayan cyborg culture, the boundaries of the 'self' are increasingly becoming blurred (many cultural theorists have concerned themselves with borders and marginality: Homi Bhabha, Paul Gilroy and Julia Kristeva). New terms are required: the 'trans-human' is halfway between the human and the 'post-human', a site of suture and marginality; the 'post-human' is an enhanced human (who may be 'post-biological'), with neurological, biological, psychological and technological enrichments.

The moment of the construction of the cyborg is a vital scene in the fantasy genre, whether it's in *Metropolis, Frankenstein* (Viktor Frankenstein cries 'it's alive!'), *The Fifth Element, Ghost In the Shell* or in the title sequence of *The Six Million Dollar Man* ('we can rebuild him' – no one asks 'why bother?'). For Raymond Bellour, movies concentrate on this primal birth scene because this is what the cinematic apparatus is always doing, substituting a simulcra for reality.[161] The reanimation of the monster, the cyborg or the human is one of cinema's specialities. It's one of cinema's (and sci-fi's) primal scenes. Cinema is, physically, a continuous resurrection: people photographed eighty years ago at 16, 18 or 24 frames per second seem to come back to life. It's the flipside of Jean-Luc Godard's remark that cinema literally films death, that the people one films will die. Also, actors speak of enjoying playing death scenes, pantomiming the mysterious, perennially fascinating moment of ultimate transition.

---

161 R. Bellour: "Ideal Hadaly", in C. Penley, 1991, 127.

DOUBLES

Doubles and *doppelgängers* is another motif in *Blade Runner*. Rick Deckard's rival is Roy Batty, but the two become doubles by the end; Deckard kills two replicants, and two save his life (Rachel and Batty); Rachel and Pris embody Western dualistic archetypes: one blonde, the other dark; one active, the other passive; one erotic, the other virginal. Rachel and Pris clearly correspond to the ancient Western mythic dualism of virgin/ whore.

There are two romantic couples as well: the bleached blond robots, Batty and Pris, and the dark-haired, more 'human' couple, Rachel and Deckard (tho' they might both be robots too). Hollywood has long had a very simple way of differentiating characters, goodies and baddies, just by hair colour. As the film progresses, Deckard and Batty move towards each other; apart from hair colour, they have similarities of costume (the high collars, for example – *Blade Runner* is a film of many costumes having high collars, including Sebastian's faded New Agey jacket, and Rachel's 1940s *film noir* fur-lined coat). By the end, they are indistinguishable from each other, with Batty ironically turning out to be the nobler one, when he saves Deckard's life.

❀

E.T.A. Hoffmann's *The Sand-Man* (1816) is another literary reference point – it influenced films such as *Metropolis* (which in turn influenced *Star Wars* and *Blade Runner*). *The Sand-Man* features an automata, Olimpia, with obvious links with the robot in *Metropolis* and the replicants in *Blade Runner*. Also in *The Sand-Man* are themes which occur in *Blade Runner*: eyes (the Sand-Man putting out people's eyes, and the automata's eyes being taken out).

Apart from E.T.A. Hoffmann, another obvious literary reference point is one of the grandmothers of all science fiction works, Mary Shelley's *Frankenstein*, with its images of creating life, playing God, subverting nature, and the monster as a shadow figure, an alter ego of the hero (compare Deckard and Batty, Tyrell and Batty).

When *Blade Runner* was first released, in 1982, some critics hated it, while many others were bemused by it: while acknowledging the impressive style of the film, the rest of it was seen as incoherent, insubstantial, and full of *film noir* private detective clichés. Brian Aldiss called it an 'overheated farrago of SF [sci-fi] crossed with private eye machismo and dragged down by pretentious sets'.162 For Pat Berman, the movie was 'like science fiction pornography – all sensation and no heart'.163

The amount of academic and cult interest that *Blade Runner* has initiated since 1982 is substantial. There are collections of essays on *Blade Runner* (*Retrofitting Blade Runner*, edited by Judith Kerman); monographs on *Blade Runner* (such as Scott Bukatman's British Film Institute Modern Classics book); and very detailed explorations of the film, such as Paul M. Sammon's *Future Noir: The Making of Blade Runner*. Some prominent critics have studied *Blade Runner*: Kaja Silverman, Slavoj Zizek, Scott Bukatman, Andrew Ross, Vivian Sobchack and Guiliana Bruno.

There have been many articles and essays on *Blade Runner* and sections in books on *Blade Runner*, such as:

▸▸ on postmodernism in *Blade Runner* (for example, Guiliana Bruno's "Ramble City"),

▸▸ on the androids/ cyborg theme (such as Donna Haraway's *Simians, Cyborgs and Women* and J.P. Telotte's *Replications: A Robotic History of the Science Fiction Film*),

▸▸ or the design of the movie (such as D. Neumann's *Film Architecture: From Metropolis to Blade Runner* and Syd Mead in Danny Peary's *Omni's Screen Flights, Screen Fantasies*),

▸▸ or on the director's cut, and so on.

Chapters on *Blade Runner* appear in books such as L. Goldberg *et al*'s *Science Fiction Filmmaking in the 1980s*, Jim Collins *et al*'s *Film Theory Goes to the Movies*, Vivian Sobchack's *Screening Space: The American Science Fiction Film*, Linda Cook and Peter Wollen's *Visual Display*, and

162 B. Aldiss: *Trillion Year Spree*, Avon Books, 1988.
163 P. Berman: *State and Columbia Record*, Columbia, July 2, 1982.

Annette Kuhn's *Alien Zone: Cultural Theory and Contemporary Science Fiction*.

Then there are pieces and chapters on:

▸ the visual effects in *Blade Runner* (such as Herb Lightman's articles, and in Christopher Finch's *Special Effects*),

▸ comic book tie-ins,

▸ novel sequels (K.W. Jeter's *Blade Runner 2: The Edge of Human* and *Replicant Night*),

▸ a fanzine (*Cityspeak*),

▸ a computer game (1997),

▸ and souvenir magazines (ed. Ira Friedman).

There are inevitably many internet sites and newsgroups dedicated to *Blade Runner*, including:

▸ Murray Chapman's *Blade Runner FAQ* page,

▸ Jon Van Oast's *2019: Off-World* page,

▸ Dan Hentschel's *Blade Runner* Homepage,

▸ Paul Brians' "Study Guide for Philip K. Dick: *Blade Runner*",

▸ Christian Rohrmeier's "Official *Blade Runner* On-line Magazine",

▸ BladeZone, an online fanzine,

▸ and Stephen Bowline and Michael Perkhofer's world-wide web page on Vangelis Papathanassiou.

Good websites for Philip K. Dick include philipkdick.com (the official site), and philipkdicksfans.com. The *Alien* series also had their own fan websites (such as *The Unofficial Alien 5 Website* and *The Alien 5 Discussion Forum*).[164]

The prospect of a sequel to *Blade Runner* was often discussed, mainly by fans (but Hollywood execs must have contemplated a sequel as the interest grew around the film in the late 1980s, and when the *Director's Cut* was released). A sequel to *Blade Runner* would be expensive, Ridley Scott acknowledged: for a start, you'd need to buy the title from the producers, which might be $2 million. And using Harrison Ford would mean $15-20 million (though it's unlikely that Ford would return).

---

164 Also: alienexperience.com and avpoe.org/amr. And when the *Alien 5* movie eventually surfaced, it was a truly dreadful Alien versus Predator piece of junk.

Critics such as Paul Sammon rave about *Blade Runner*, saying it

> not only revealed an *adult* narrative and *complex* characters (subtle, dramatically wrenching ones at that), it also evidenced a *thematic* complexity every bit as intricate as its much discussed *visual* complexity. (1996, xvii)

In his 1999 book on Ridley Scott's cinema, Paul Sammon attested that *Blade Runner* is a

> haunting, hypnotic, harrowing achievement, one whose overwhelming visuals are strongly linked to its ideas – provocative, multi-textured ones, each subversively embedded in the understructure of what appears to be a mainstream Hollywood product. *Blade Runner* may be narratively flawed and (at times) precariously self-indulgent, but it also remains one of the truly lustrous jewels in Scott's creative crown, a cinematic milestone whose basic integrity, form of imagination and ideo-logical sophistication forever altered the face of con-temporary science fiction cinema. (1999, 73).

There is a truly amazing amount of critical material surrounding *Blade Runner*. 'In the world of blockbuster studies, *Blade Runner* nuts rank second only to *Alien* scholars in their devotion to the cause, although they are 50 percent more likely to use the word "hyper-reality"', as Tom Shone put it (119).[165]

Sometimes it seems that the amount of critical attention that *Blade Runner* has generated is out of proportion with the film itself. It's a good movie, but is it really *that* good? Whatever, *Blade Runner* is certainly a movie that film critics and fans and PhD students love to discuss. *Blade Runner* is the modern *Citizen Kane*, a film that is widely taken to be one of the highpoints of contemporary cinema.

And the influence of *Blade Runner* in contemporary cinema is huge, too – most obviously in its look and design,

---

165 All of those elements which critics have discussed *ad infinitum* in *Blade Runner* – the racial, ethnic, feminist and cyborg aspects of the replicants, for instance – are not essential to the plot, which is basically: the replicants are robots which Deckard has to hunt down and destroy.

but also in its themes and characters. And the impact of *Blade Runner* on pop music and MTV and fashion has been enormous, too. The long coats, the black leather jackets, the eye-liner, the rain and smoke – you might be at a Cure or Gary Numan gig.

Blade Runner is one of those films that have been quoted many times in pop music, within songs – like *2001: A Space Odyssey* or *The Wizard of Oz*. It's a movie that's loved by musicians and composers – not least because of its marvellous soundtrack by Vangelis.

NEGATIVE CRITICISM OF *BLADE RUNNER*

Some negative criticism might include seeing *Blade Runner* as a flawed film, where the near-faultless camerawork, visual effects, lighting and set design are marred by the conventional hard-boiled cop story and *film noir* characters, the Hollywood romance, and some sexist stances.

The scene where the snake woman replicant, Zhora, is killed by Deckard is one such moment of grotesque violence: the near-naked character is dressed in see-through plastic fetish wear;[166] she is shot on L.A.'s streets, running away from Deckard, a woman being shot from behind, and a woman who's working in a lowly position in the entertainment industry ('[e]ven the most cynical forties *film noir* hero didn't do that', said actress Joanna Cassidy [FN, 157]). She crashes into a row of plate glass windows (and was also going to carry on and be hit by a bus).

Zhora's death occurs in Sam Peckinpah-like slow motion, accompanied by the quiet washes of Vangelis's synthesizers. The blood spatters inside the plastic coat. It still has a creepy, exploitative aspect to it for me.[167]

Another serious flaw in *Blade Runner* is the climactic battle between Deckard and Batty, which on some viewings seems dragged out for far too long. Rutger Hauer's Batty is

166 Joanna Cassidy's make-up of body paint and sequins took 3 hours to apply by 4 people, according to make-up artist Marvin Westmore (FN, 153).
167 And I was unhappy about showing that part of the film to my students when we went through the movie scene-by-scene. It's kinda repulsive.

played far too camp to be fearsome, while Sean Young and Daryl Hannah often elicit only indifference. (Writers Hampton Fancher and David Peoples recalled the duel didn't seem big enough to climax the movie, but they were blown away when they saw how the filmmakers had done it).

The protagonists, as believable human (or cyborg) characters, fail to encourage empathy, and are swamped by the filmmakers' overpowering emphasis on the *mise-en-scène* and design. *Blade Runner* is not an emotionally engaging movie like, say, *Pelle the Conqueror* or *Fanny and Alexander*. The puzzle and detection aspects of the film (apparently added by David Peoples at Harrison Ford's behest), were also routine: Deckard searching apartments and finding snake scales and photos; Deckard interrogating Rachel (though using the new addition of the Voigt-Kampff machine).

Other aspects came straight out of *film noir*: the hard-bitten, alienated, morally-dubious detective; the (futuristic, russet-hued) trenchcoat; hanging around in bars; drinking whisky; cigarettes; the jaded police captain; the *femme fatale*; the L.A. setting; the blinds; the fans; and the voiceover.

Quite a bit of *Blade Runner* was patched up in the editing suite – more than one might think. Or maybe it's because the mistakes or the gluing over the seams is more obvious than in some films. Sure, there are mistakes in every movie ever made, but in *Blade Runner* the film editing and the sound editing isn't quite slick enough to cover up the holes. There are a few scenes, for instance, where dialogue has been added in post-production – the scene where Deckard takes the snake scale to the Cambodian seller (Kimiko Hiroshige), for instance. There's hardly a shot of the woman speaking in close-up, always a giveaway that a scene has been rewritten and dubbed after it was shot. Other instances of awkward editing and crude post-production include the scene with the Egyptian animal trader, Abdul Ben-Hassan.[168] (Some of those errors were corrected in *The*

---

168 That came about partly because the producers wanted to clarify the information in the scene, and the scene was rewritten and looped, as editor Terry Rawlings explained (FN, 148). 'That didn't really work, though, did it?' Rawlings added.

Final Cut).

Twenty years later, films like *Blade Runner* would be made with thirty cameras running simultaneously, so some coverage or close-ups would be shot which could cover up mistakes (such as the tried and tested method of cutting to a meaningless close-up of some minor action with the hands to cover an ellipse in the action or an actor's flubbed line).

❁

While there's plenty for critics following postmodernist, semiotic, psychoanalytic and other cultural theories to get their teeth into in *Blade Runner,* second wave feminists have much to complain about. *Blade Runner* is a very masculinist movie in many respects. It's a patriarchal culture, with all the key positions of authority being taken by men (cops, captains, replicant leaders, C.E.O.s). And the three most prominent women in the film are all robots. One is a dancer, one is a hooker, and one is a secretary.[169]

Blade Runner's not, in short, a movie with characters that second wave feminists can rave about (like the other Philip K. Dick adaptions). Third wave or postmodern feminists, though, can find much in *Blade Runner* to explore – the notions of identity, of cyborg status, of hyperspace, and so on.

FEMME FATALES AND 19TH CENTURY ART

The women in *Blade Runner*, Pris, Rachel and Zhora, recall the *femme fatales* in 19th century art, in painters such as Gustave Moreau, Edvard Munch, Félicien Rops, Odilon Redon, Jean Delville and Franz von Stuck. The *femme fatale* was one of the main types of women in 19th century European painting: there were other incarnations or versions of the same basic type: the woman as death, as a prostitute, as a dominatrix, a temptress, a queen, a warrior, an Amazon,

169 No mothers, carers, partners, wives or other types of women in *Blade Runner,* beyond the women in the bar, and the old woman who identifies the snake scale, as Mary Doane points out. But the concept of the maternal is still present (1999, 28). The 6th replicant, Mary, would have been a mother figure.

and so on. Note that Zhora's stage name in 'Miss Salomé', Salomé being a key 19th century *femme fatale*, a version of the erotic, castrating woman.

The *femme fatale* type neatly melds sex and death, desire and fear, contact and loss, for the (male) artist. She appears in figures from myth and history such as Medusa, Salomé, Delilah, Jezebel, Judith, Lilith, Ninue (the lover of Merlin), Venus, Helen of Troy, La Belle Dame Sans Merci and Cleopatra. These female 'types' combined beauty with death, immense power and all manner of sadistic, masochistic and fetishistic fantasies. These are the women who will whip one to death, if one wishes, as in Leopold Sacher-Masoch's *Venus in Furs*. Easy to see how the punk blonde Pris corresponds with the powerful warrior or Amazon type, a teasing dominatrix for Deckard, who leaps on his shoulders and strangles him between her thighs. With her stockings, mini-skirt, thick make-up and bleached hair, Pris is a male fantasy, a prostitute, literally a 'love machine', with a penchant for kinky, fetishistic sex. The robot woman as sex machine is of course another common trope in science fiction.

Rachel can be seen as the 19th century flipside of the 'holy whore' figure of Cleopatra, Medusa, Venus and Salomé, the 'passive virgin' or 'good woman' type, repressed, dreamy, waiting. In Symbolist art she is the pale, drowned Ophelia in John Everett Millais' painting (1851-52, Tate Gallery, London), or the wistful madonnas of Pre-Raphaelite art (particularly in the work of Edward Burne-Jones, Millais, Holman Hunt and Dante Gabriel Rossetti), and in Gustave Moreau's softly dreaming images of *Sappho* (1872, Victoria & Albert Museum, London).

Zhora, the snake dancer, corresponds with the ancient associations between women and death, women and snakes. Painters such as Franz von Stuck produced famous depictions of *femme fatales* with snakes. Stuck's most popular image, which he painted 18 times, was *Vice* (1894, Cologne): in near-darkness, a muscley, nude woman reclines on her belly, the dark form of a snake curling around her. Her head turned to the viewer, wearing a lascivious smile, she holds her breast.

In Franz von Stuck's famous picture of the same theme (*Sin*, 1893, Neue Pinakothek, Munich), glowing female flesh again appears out of darkness. In *Sin*, female nudity is the focus of the image: the woman's breasts, belly and abdomen are glowing whitely, while her face and clothes are shrouded in shadow. So popular were Stuck's serpent-women, rows of seats were put in front of the picture for the visitors at the 1893 Munich Secession exhibition.

In *Blade Runner*, Jordan Cronenweth's baroque, shadowy lighting and design also looks decidedly 19th century: the browns and sepias of the Tyrell Corporation interiors, for example, recall the Egyptian and Babylonian architecture of Gustave Moreau's paintings (such as his densely layered, incredibly detailed image of *Salomé* in the Hammer Collection in Los Angeles). As yet, no movie has captured the intensity of detail in artists such as Moreau and Gustave Doré. If only!

❁

Watching *Blade Runner* again recently, I was struck by how much of the film is taken up by the romantic plot: indeed, it's not a subplot, but a dual plot with the narrative of Deckard hunting down the replicants. In short, *Blade Runner* is a very *romantic* movie: it's about a guy and his girl, after all (like a lot of Raymond Chandleresque detective fiction, too). It's Bogart and Bacall again (though, sorry to say, Sean Young ain't quite Lauren Bacall). That was very much from Hampton Fancher's drafts of the script.

Because when Deckard isn't hunting down replicants, he's holed up with Rachel in his apartment. It's striking just how much of *Blade Runner* really is a romantic love story, with the narrative device of keeping the lovers apart this time being the slight problem that one of them isn't human. Or, if you buy into the theory that Deckard is also a replicant, you've got a love story between two robots. That's bizarre, certainly, but not in science fiction, or in science fiction cinema. There are many examples of machines, computers or robots wishing to become human (it's rarely the other way around – who'd want to be a robot?). The 1999 film *Bicentennial Man*, starring Robin Williams and directed by Chris Columbus, featured a robot hankering after humanity, including romantic love. And the 2001 film *A.I. Artificial Intelligence* also covered similar territory, with a child, played by Haley Joel Osment, wanting to become a real boy, as in *Pinocchio.*

THE INFLUENCE OF *BLADE RUNNER*

Probably the most influential aspect of *Blade Runner* was its *mis-en-scène*, copied in many subsequent films, such as *Judge Dredd* (1995), *Brazil* (Terry Gilliam, 1985), the *Batman* series, *Twelve Monkeys* (Terry Gilliam, 1995), *Cyborg* (Albert Pyun, 1989), *Total Recall* (Paul Verhoeven, 1990), *Akira* (Katsuhiro Otomo, 1988), *Strange Days* (Kathryn Bigelow, 1995), *Johnny Mnemonic* (Robert Longo, 1995), *The Salute of the Jugger* (David Peoples, 1990), the *Matrix* series, and *The Fifth Element* (Luc Besson, 1997).[170]

BATMAN.

For my money, Warners' *Batman* films are among the most captivating and luscious of fantasy visions in contemporary cinema (the four movies, 1989-1997, not the recycled franchise from 2005's *Batman Begins* onwards). The depictions of Gotham City – futuristic, nightmarish, squalid, multi-level and multi-ethnic – are easily the equal of the highpoints of contemporary cinema's cities, whether in *Blade Runner*, the *Star Wars* saga, *A.I.*, *Total Recall* or *The Fifth Element*.

Shot in Britain at Pinewood Studios, 1989's *Batman* was an epic of production design, for which Anton Furst rightly won the Oscar.[171] *Batman* was shot by Roger Pratt.[172] The backlot at Pinewood was transformed into a

170 Other flicks linked to Phil Dick's work include *A Nightmare On Elm Street, Mulholland Drive, Fight Club, Vanilla Sky, Donnie Darko, Videodrome, Existenz, Being John Malkovich, Adaptation, Eternal Sunshine of the Spotless Mind, Dark City, The Truman Show, Gattaca* and *Memento*.
171 Anton Furst was assisted by protegé Nigel Phelps, who went on to design *Judge Dredd, Alien Resurrection, In Dreams* and *The Bone Collector*.
172 Roger Pratt's previous credits included *Brazil*, a film which has affinities with *Batman* and *Blade Runner* – a nightmarish, futuristic city, models, paranoia, and Pratt's later work included *The Fisher King* and *Twelve Monkeys.*

vision of Gotham City as a dark, shadowy recreation a *film noirish* 1940s New York, a slice of Art Deco American Gothic, brownstones, and fascist pomp.

Director Tim Burton didn't want to shoot on real New York locations, as *Superman* (1978) had done. He wanted something extreme and operatic, specially created for the characters, and to recreate the look of the comic books. Burton said he forbade the use of neon, which would be too reminiscent of *Blade Runner*, and persuaded the production designers to try for something that didn't follow *Blade Runner*'s highly influential style.[173] The result was that *Batman*, with its combination of Roger Pratt's stunning cinematography, Anton Furst's designs, Bob Ringwood's outrageous (and very influential) costumes and Burton's vision, is probably the best-looking blockbuster of the 1980s and 1990s.[174]

BRAZIL.

Brazil (Terry Gilliam, 1985) is one of the most satisfying post-*Blade Runner* movies. The exaggerated dystopian vision of Universal's *Brazil* recalls *Blade Runner* (and *Mad Max*),[175] and clearly influenced later sci-fi and fantasy films like *Delicatessen*, *Alien: Resurrection*, *The Matrix* and *The Fifth Element*.

Although a film such as *Blade Runner* was regarded as the utter highpoint of (postmodern) production design in contemporary cinema, the vision of the city of the future which cultural critics continue to deify, *Brazil* was perhaps more inventive, more extraordinary, and more persuasive. The inventiveness of *Brazil* is overwhelming. And *Brazil*, like *Blade Runner*, hasn't aged at all (the breakneck pace of the

173 Like previous futuristic films such as *Batman* and *The Event Horizon*, *Minority Report* also studiously avoided the plethora of neons of *Blade Runner* (with which *Minority Report* would be inevitably compared, being another Philip K. Dick adaption). *Minority Report* did use *Blade Runner*'s giant hoardings and billboards, though (but they were animated holograms projected onto buildings and structures).

174 However, Francis Coppola's *Bram Stoker's Dracula* would be a strong contender for the most beautifully crafted blockbuster, with outstanding lensing by Michael Balhaus, art direction by Andrew Precht, and production design by Thomas Saunders and Dante Ferretti.

175 The influence of the *Mad Max* films is often under-estimated – and not only in their look, but in the big box office returns they generated (and the first *Mad Max* was very low budget, by Hollywood standards).

editing certainly helps).

TWELVE MONKEYS.

Twelve Monkeys (Universal, 1995) was a sci-fi thriller written by David and Jan Peoples (Peoples had co-written *Blade Runner*). Although known as a movie directed by Terry Gilliam, *Twelve Monkeys* is much more significant for its witty, clever, intricate screenplay, the narrative is far more satisfying than *Blade Runner*. It features familiar 1990s sci-fi themes: time travel, paranoia, a post-apocalyptic vision (a deadly virus which wipes out most of humanity), paranoia, Big Brother, an individual against the world, and a romance. Chris Marker's 1962 film *La Jetée* was the starting-point for *Twelve Monkeys*.[176]

Two big Hollywood stars (Bruce Willis and Brad Pitt) appeared, with Madeleine Stowe as the romantic interest, Dr Railly, who tries to save the hero, James Cole.[177] *Twelve Monkeys* was impressive on many levels: it had a beautifully worked-out script, which tied together a wealth of motifs and tiny details, cleverly fusing foreshadowed events and pay-offs. And the screenplay of *Twelve Monkeys* pushed the narrative along at a cracking pace.

There was a deep-seated passion, anger (and sometimes despair) at the heart of *Twelve Monkeys*, a romantic, humanistic view of life. What gave the film its emotional power was the intensity with which Cole pursued his quest. Here, the standard fusion of two plot strands of his quest – saving the world and heterosexual romance – were deftly, convincingly performed. In *Twelve Monkeys*, Cole's involvement with Railly was critical to the central plot of time travel to save the world from the virus. She was the only one who believed in him, and who helped him.

---

176 *La Jetée* was a powerful photo essay, essentially a series of black-and-white still photographs accompanied by a voiceover and sound effects. *La Jetée* concerned a man being sent through time in a scientific experiment, in a post-apocalyptic world; the *mise-en-scène* was expertly evoked by shadows, *film noir* lighting and deft editing.
177 Cole was a familiar Hollywood lead: the reluctant hero, violent but basically good, flawed but redeemed in the end.

THE MATRIX.

Warner Brothers' big sci-fi adventure series of the late 1990s and early 2000s, the *Matrix* trilogy, clearly drew on *Blade Runner* and the fiction of Philip K. Dick (the paranoia, the Big Brother aspects, the altered realities, etc), and stole wholesale from *Ghost In the Shell*. Cultural theorists and fan boys get very gooey about the *Matrix* films, but for me, beyond some cool designs and fun action sequences (overseen by the wonderful Yuen Woo-Ping, the grand master of martial arts choreographers), I can't think of much to say about them.

THE FIFTH ELEMENT.

Films such as *The Fifth Element* (Columbia/ Gaumont, 1997) were practically *hommages* to *Blade Runner*: movies are full of tensions, and in *The Fifth Element* there were conflicts between director Luc Besson's French *cinéma du look* approach, with its emphasis on cool visual style, and the Hollywood blockbuster, with its big budget, visual effects, spectacle, action and mainstream star (Bruce Willis).

The Fifth Element built upon *Blade Runner*'s future city look, with a New York City crammed with yellow taxis and NYPD cars flying between the skyscrapers; Willis's Korben Dallas was a kind of Deckard character (rebellious, a loner and outsider – but basically good); who's divorced, childless (how few action heroes are lumbered with children!); gets 'phoned up and berrated by his possessive mother; and wins the girl at the end.

There was also a replicant/ cyborg plot, with the female superbeing character Leeloo (Milla Jovovich, at the time Monsieur Besson's partner) being rebuilt in a scientific laboratory (she's the missing 'fifth element'.) Other *Blade Runner* aspects of *The Fifth Element* included the casting of Brion James, who played Leon the replicant in *Blade Runner*, and having Dallas being served food from a kind of flying Chinese junk, recalling the advertizing blimps, noodle bars and Chinatown setting in *Blade Runner*.[178]

---

178 Another connection between *Blade Runner* and *The Fifth Element*: it used Moebius as a designer, who had influenced the look of the Philip K. Dick film. (Moebius and Jean-Claude Mézières were comic book artists whom Besson had enjoyed as a youth).

However, *The Fifth Element* was a postmodern *mélange* of earlier sci-fi and fantasy films (*2001: A Space Odyssey* and *Blade Runner* included), which added nothing new to the genre. There were shape-changing alien baddies (courtesy of CGI and masks, and recalling the aliens in *Men In Black*, made the same year), a psychopathic villain, Zorg (Gary Oldman), hardware (such as an enormous *Rambo*-style gun that could deliver bullets, arrows, flames, freezing ice, nets, etc), big sets (the opera house interior, for example), amazing costumes, lightspeed space travel, a *Star Wars*-style space battle, a chase through the upper storeys of New York City (oddly, to the sound of North African *rai* pop, by the wonderful Cheb Khaled, a distinctly 'French', cosmopolitan choice), and a plot involving: ancient races (as in *Stargate* and the *Indiana Jones* films), Milla Jovovich as the reconstituted 'fifth element' needed to save the world, a search for the MacGuffin (the four 'stones' of the four elements), concessions to political correctness (Tiny List Jr's President was black, secondary characters such as Chris Tucker's Rudy Rhod and Tricky were black), and an attack by an alien planet. As in other disaster films of the mid-1990s (*Armageddon, Deep Impact, Asteroid*), Earth was again threatened by an asteroid hurtling towards it.

AKIRA.

But while Western films such as *Batman, Brazil* and *The Fifth Element* took up some of *Blade Runner*'s ideas and visuals, it was the Japanese animation industry that really explored them to the full (is there a major Japanese science fiction *animé* that *doesn't* reference *Blade Runner*? No).[179] Three are worth mentioning here – three of the most extraordinary movies ever made.[180] (I would also include anything by Hayao Miyazaki).[181]

Akira (1988) was one of the biggest-selling of Japanese

[179] For many Japanese *animé* filmmakers, *Blade Runner* has been a major inspiration, a storehouse of possibilities. No matter what you think of *Blade Runner*, its importance for Japanese *animé* is enormous. *Blade Runner* has influenced *Akira, Patlabor, Appleseed, Legend of the Overfiend,* and *Ghost In the Shell.*

[180] *Cowboy Bebop, Final Fantasy* and *Evangelion* would be others.

[181] But I have recently published a book about Miyazaki, I won't include his matchless movies here.

animé films overseas (that and *Legend of the Overfiend*). If you've seen an *animé*, it's probably *Akira*. *Akira* was the baby of Katsuhiro Otomo: he directed the movie, wrote the script, designed it, and it was based on his *manga* comic strip (published in *Young* magazine, 1982-90).[182]

While film critics have raved endlessly about the visualization of futuristic cities in movies such as *Blade Runner*, *Akira* went far beyond them. *Akira* was set in a post-apocalyptic Tokyo (called Neo-Tokyo), a city rebuilding itself. The design work on *Akira* was staggering: the acreage of detail in every shot, the inventiveness of the locations, the combinations of modern and postmodern architecture, the staging of the action, the choice of camera angles, and the framing. This was filmmaking of a very high quality and power of imagination. If you haven't seen *Akira*, you *must* see it.

Like many sci-fi films of the 1980s, *Akira* explored a post-apocalyptic society, a social breakdown combined with draconian measures to keep the populace in check, with the military taking over from politicians in policing the city (a common theme in Japanimation). *Akira* pitted young motorbike gangs against the military-industrial complex, against scientists, committees and generals. Politically, *Akira* is very sophisticated – it makes the politics of *Blade Runner* look pathetically simplistic.

There was a strong messianic, religious strand to *Akira*: a project experimenting with telepathy and supernormal powers in children goes out of control. One of the biker gang members, Tetsuo Shima, becomes super-powerful, in the traditional *animé* fashion (which means lots of super-hero devastation); and, at the end of the film, in the apocalyptic climax, the real, long-awaited Akira arrives – glimpsed as a young boy enveloped in white light.

Nuclear holocaust haunts *Akira*, reflecting the time of its creation – the mid-1980s, when anxiety over an escalation of arms resulting in an atomic conflict was intense. There's also a disturbing undercurrent in *Akira*, because it's made in and set in modern Japan, the only country (thus

---

182 Otomo's follow-up to *Akira*, *Steam-boy*, eventually appeared in 2004, after many delays.

far) that has been bombed by nuclear weapons. This gives the images at the end of *Akira*, of a colossal hemisphere of white light that expands outwards and eats up the city, an added *frisson* of despair and horror.

Akira doesn't disappoint as an action movie: lots of motorcycle chases, fights between rival biker gangs, gun battles (though not too many), and extraordinary scenes of destruction as Tetsuo chews up Neo-Tokyo. And there's a genuine epic dimension in *Akira*, which's lacking in many action-adventure films ('big' doesn't mean 'epic'). *Akira* is certainly as big, loud, pacey (and silly) as the best action-adventure movies, but there's a genuine mythic grandeur to the piece. It derives partly from *Akira* being animation: it can be much more extravagant, visually, than a live-action film, it can go places, use camera angles and compositions, that are impossible in live-action (even with digital embellishments).

GHOST IN THE SHELL.

One of the most impressive of all movies that developed science fiction cinema from *Blade Runner* is *Ghost In the Shell* (1995), a masterpiece of Japanese animation, directed by Mamoru Oshii and scripted by Oshii and Kazunori Ito, from the classic, highly idiosyncratic and wholly original *manga* by Masamune Shirow. Certainly *Ghost In the Shell* is one of the finest of its kind – and it's a sci-fi action-adventure movie that can hold its own with the best of them, whether in live action (*Total Recall, Minority Report, Westworld, Planet of the Apes*), or in Japanese animation (*Laputa: Castle In the Sky, Legend of the Overfiend, Akira*, etc).[183] On its own terms, which is how the best movies operate, *Ghost In the Shell* works like gangbusters. Although well-known in *animé* circles, it really

---

183 As well as the two *Ghost In the Shell* feature films, there is a *Ghost In the Shell* animated series (2002) – *Ghost In the Shell: Stand Alone Complex* (with a number of series within series, too). *Ghost In the Shell: Stand Alone Complex* is one of the most accomplished of all Japanese *animé* TV shows. Certainly in terms of issues and themes, it goes way, way beyond *Blade Runner*.

deserves to be much better known.[184] Simply in terms of animation, it's a masterwork.[185]

Ghost In the Shell centred on the Major, Motoko Kusanagi (beautifully voiced by Atsuko Tanaka), a cyborg cop (and, yes, she just happens to have a pneumatic body, with big boobs and a tight ass, and has to take her clothes off from time to time – but only to do her work, you understand.[186] And, yes, the plot does explain what her body is, a cyborg's shell, but don't let that fool you – it's tits and ass. And there's stuff with thermoptic camouflage suits and other technofetishism to explain what is basically a nude woman kicking butt. Show *Ghost In the Shell* to your girlfriends, your sisters, your mothers, your daughters, and they'll look at the nude cyborg Motoko Kusanagi and shake their heads and laugh – *Ghost In the Shell* is totally boys' stuff).

Yes, *Ghost In the Shell* teases and titillates the audience – 'fan service', as it's sometimes called, though the term 'entertainment' covers it all: the credit sequence, which's fabulous, involves the naked cyborg being prepared for action, dipped in baths of different kinds, and the first action scene has Kusanagi up on the roof of some skyscraper in Hong Kong (not Tokyo this time, altho' it's actually meant to be Newport City), just about to launch herself over the edge. And what does she do before becoming the Android Cop Supreme? Takes her clothes off! Nope, not even Arnold Schwarzenegger or Bruce Willis or Harrison Ford went this far. In Japanese *anime*, it's always best to take your clothes off before leaping into action.

Ghost In the Shell was stuffed with imaginative ideas,

184 According to producer Joel Silver, super-nerds the Wachowski brothers (or should that be brother and sister?) showed him *Ghost In the Shell* to indicate the kind of look they were going for. *The Matrix* (1999) turned out to be virtually a remake of both *Ghost In the Shell* and *Akira*, with some scenes seemingly lifted wholesale, and details right down to the use of green, or the computer read-outs against black. Director Mamoru Oshii wasn't so bothered – he acknowledged that everyone takes from everyone else's work, and the parts employed in *The Matrix* were well done.
185 Computers and digital networks are a major thematic component as well as the primary theme of the *Ghost In the Shell* movies. It's all about humans and technology again – which may be Japanese *anime*'s chief theme (in some *anime*, for instance, the theme is given an ecological slant, as in the movies of Hayao Miyazaki).
186 The poster for *Ghost In the Shell* features an image of the naked Kusanagi, with her breasts prominent.

spectacular and intricately detailed visuals, and brilliant staging of action (the budget was 600 million Yen = $6 million). It was sci-fi, the usual futuristic city and techno-logically advanced society. Yet, incredibly, *Ghost In the Shell* managed to explore serious metaphysical issues, like the best science fiction – such as the relation between humanity and artificial intelligence, between bodies and cyborgs, and between machines and global capitalism.

Director Mamoru Oshii has expressed his admiration for *Blade Runner*, which his cinema clearly draws on. I would argue that not only is the 1995 *Ghost In the Shell* a worthy successor to *Blade Runner*, it also, along with *Ghost In the Shell 2: Innocence* and the *Ghost In the Shell* TV series, tops *Blade Runner*: in some of its filmmaking, its style, and its visuals, and certainly in the elegance and depth of its metaphysical and philosophical explorations. *Blade Runner* suggests a welter of philosophical material but doesn't deliver it. Instead, it has taken 100s of critics and commentators and PhD students to elaborate on what *Blade Runner* hinted at. And it is those philosophical speculations in *Blade Runner*, and similar movies about artificial life, like *Solaris*, *Bicentennial Man* and *A.I.*, that the *Ghost In the Shell* movies have developed to a far richer and more sophisticated degree.

Ghost In the Shell was another of those movies – like *Solaris*, *A.I.* or *Blade Runner* – that explored what it means to be human. Can a machine or a computer have a soul? Can an android have a human soul implanted in it? Does self-awareness in a machine equate to identity in humans? Can machines have children, with variety and individuality, or merely copies of themselves? (This was one of the futuristic notions of *Ghost In the Shell* – the 'ghost' or soul in a metal shell. Many of those questions have been central to the fiction of Philip K. Dick, and the movies based on his work).

And in *Ghost In the Shell* those questions really were part of the fabric of the piece, and weren't pretentious or pompous at all. Partly because from the beginning, *Ghost In the Shell* announces that it's not going to be your usual shoot-em-up cyborg cop action-adventure movie. It's going to stop and *think*. Really think! Wow. A film that thinks!

Ghost In the Shell is highly successful in depicting computerization on screen. A difficult, complex and abstract thing, but *Ghost In the Shell* gets closer than most movies – especially in the fusion of computer read-outs, and those streams of green numbers, and the layers of coloured digital images sliding over each other. Because in this movie, as in the sequel, the 'check-mate' really occurs inside computer networks. So *Ghost In the Shell* is really *the* great cyber-thriller, a movie in which the cyberspace/ cyborg/ hi-tech element really is fundamental to the plot and the theme (and the characters, who are all technologically augmented in some way or another).

There was also time in *Ghost In the Shell* for a few slower-paced montages, with dialogue and action replaced by mesmerizing (predominantly static) images set to music. The stand-out slow-paced montage was the canal sequence: highly unusual in an action movie, or a cop thriller, it comprised elaborate and beautiful images of downtown Hong Kong, focussing on the canal area (essentially a mood piece, it was dominated by Kenji Kawai's fabulous music).

And then there's the animation: *Ghost In the Shell* was mounted very much in the *Akira* style: moody images of a futuristic city coloured in blues and blacks, with many scenes taking place at night. Cars, buildings, props, weapons and bodies were sleek, professional, hi-tech. It's one of those cities of the future with soaring skyscrapers, multi-lane free-ways and bridges, neons and signage everywhere, and dingy back streets and alleys (for the chases on foot).

The romance in *Ghost In the Shell* is between two cyborgs – Kusanagi and Batou (Batou is not a full android, but he's close). Or it's a romance between a guy with plenty of cyborgian embellishments and a cyborg. And that's weird – but no weirder than *Blade Runner* (it's sick, as Rutger Hauer put it – Deckard and Rachel – *yeeuuwww!*).

The sequel, *Ghost In the Shell 2: Innocence* (Mamoru Oshii, 2004), was similarly wonderful to look at, with some divinely accomplished animation (in particular the fusion of 2-D and 3-D elements). At the level of detail, *Ghost In the Shell 2* was sumptuous animation (the budget was high for a

Japanese animated movie, at 2,000 million Yen (= $20 million). In the West, it would've cost a zillion times that). *Ghost In the Shell 2* was entered in the best movie category at the Cannes Film Festival.

So many aspects of *Ghost In the Shell 2* were superlative. There was so much going in *Ghost In the Shell 2*, so much that was astonishing visually (and musically – Kenji Kawai was back composing the music). For Mamoru Oshii, the story in the *Ghost In the Shell* sequel wasn't complicated at all: 'it may look like a confusing movie as I have been told by many people, but to me, *it is a simple love story*' (my emphasis).187

Ghost In the Shell 2: Innocence is another version of *Blade Runner* – right from the opening shot, it's *Blade Runner* all over again. Mamoru Oshi has never got over seeing the 1982 Warners movie (like so many other Japanese animators).

The police plot of *Ghost In the Shell 2: Innocence* is actually *Blade Runner*, isn't it? Cops tracking down robots that've gone nuts and started killing people. That the robots're hookers brings out what *Blade Runner* tended to cover up (Pris, for instance, is referred to as a 'pleasure model', and is clearly eroticized in her costume and look. But the movie is curiously reticent when it came to portraying sex).

LEGEND OF THE OVERFIEND.

Aside from *Akira*, the *Legend of the Overfiend* series (1987-1997) is one of the most remarkable examples of filmmaking in the contemporary era, which makes almost everything that Hollywood and Europe turns out look pitifully tame. *Legend of the Overfiend* is a mass of phallic, testosterone, hormone-driven, Japanese *anime* fantasy.

Legend of the Overfiend is disarming and compelling because of the sheer intensity and rapidity of the imagery. The film barely lets up for a moment, careening from one gory superhero battle to the next. The comicbook style of Japanese *manga* is exaggerated to the point of total optical saturation: it's all bright colours, panoramic views of Osaka

187 M. Oshii, in M. Koepke, "Fantastic Phantasms", *Hour*, 2004.

and Tokyo at night, giant full moons, human figures that soar through the air, demonic faces with livid red eyes, phallic tentacles hundreds of feet long plunging into flesh, and never-ending, violent corporeal transformations. For some, it's porn, sexist, violent, for others (myself included), it's visionary and boundlessly inventive filmmaking.

In *Akira*, *Ghost In the Shell*, and *Legend of the Overfiend* and similar Japanese animated films, the futuristic cityscapes of *Blade Runner* are expanded and energized. Above the city lights and skyscrapers in *Blade Runner* flying vehicles dreamily float along, accompanied by washes of Vangelis's melancholy synthesizers. In *Akira*, *Ghost In the Shell*, *Legend of the Overfiend* and other similar Japanese movies, mile-long tentacles hurtle through the air, storms rage, humans transform into gigantic demons, and whole sections of the cities are exploding or being crushed.

In the air above Los Angeles in *Blade Runner*, the worst that can happen is getting a bit of dust in your giant eye as you stare hypnotized through the spinner's windshield at distant flashing lights. In *Legend of the Overfiend*, if you're up in the air, you're going to be penetrated in every orifice and all over your body by speeding tentacles, or you'll be blown to pieces, or you might be fucked by some two hundred foot demon.

BLADE RUNNER TODAY

Today, *Blade Runner* can appear a little slow: made now, it would be much faster, with more action beats, and the action beats would be much louder, more violent, and much longer. Ironically, it would probably be a *longer* film, though: because despite editing being more rapid in contemporary cinema (i.e., shot lengths are shorter on average), Hollywood films are actually longer on average: instead of one hour fifty minutes or whatever *Blade Runner* is, it would probably be two hours twenty minutes, or even more (which's far too long, I reckon).188

The replicants mutineering on some spaceship (like a slave uprising) would undoubtedly be the action beat that would open *Blade Runner* if it was produced today: a long, complex visual effects scene costing 20 million, it would involve lots of gunplay and explosions and deaths, and would show the replicants in action as nasty critters. Having Leon shoot Holden in the Tyrell pyramid just isn't quite as juicy.

A scene introducing Deckard in a stylish and memorable fashion would be necessary, too: in the film he's standing in the street reading a newspaper, waiting for his food to be cooked. He could be anybody, and that static scene doesn't do much to describe his character.

A contemporary version of *Blade Runner* would surely introduce the character in action. An early draft of the script had Deckard showing up at a farm and wasting the farmer, who turns out to be a replicant. That's better, because it shows Deckard doing his job: in the film as is, Deckard doesn't get to show what sort of a blade runner he actually is until halfway through the movie, when he shoots and kills Zhora.

It's the stately pace of *Blade Runner* that would be altered today, that some newer viewers coming to the film might find just too s-l-o-w.189

In many circles, *Blade Runner* will be regarded as one of the great science fiction movies, as well as one of the great films of recent times. Maybe. But if it is a masterpiece, it is also flawed. *Blade Runner* is staggeringly good, but there are flaws: the plot creaks, there are clichés, the casting isn't quite spot on (Sean Young), and some of the performances are routine. *Blade Runner* isn't an out-and-out classic, like *Citizen Kane*, *The Seven Samurai* or *Contempt*.

---

188 On shot lengths and changing fashions in Hollywood cinema, see David Bordwell's wonderful book *The Way Hollywood Tells It*.
189 I've used *Blade Runner* with GCSE students in the U.K. (16 year-olds), back in 1992, when we looked at a bit of *Blade Runner* each week across 13 weeks. I just about got away with it: it was a slow movie for the classroom, but the spellbinding visuals kept them hooked. (I also used *Tess* (1979) – what was I thinking?! A girlie 19th century costume drama with a female lead in a room of restless, working-class 16 year-olds!).

AFTERWORD

Philip K. Dick's stories have formed the basis of some highly entertaining movies, and two solid gold classics of science fiction cinema: *Blade Runner* and *Total Recall*. *Blade Runner* is of course a film in the top ten lists of many filmmakers and fans. It has an afterlife up there with classics like *Singin' In the Rain*, *Bicycle Thieves* or *Jules et Jim*. It's a movie that keeps going on and on.

Some of the Philip K. Dick pictures are distinctly minor – *Next*, *Screamers*, *Paycheck*, *Impostor* – but they are enjoyable for at least one viewing. And a movie such as *Minority Report* is so dense visually it demands repeated screenings. But not every Phil Dick adaption can be a beloved film like *Blade Runner*, like not every new comedy flick can be *Duck Soup* or *The General*.

The adaptions of Philip K. Dick's fiction started out on a very high point – with *Blade Runner*. And the sub-genre shows no sign of slowing up. Indeed, since 2002, the year of *Minority Report* and *Impostor*, versions of Dick's stories keep coming, making him one of the most adapted of sci-fi authors, way ahead of Arthur C. Clarke, Isaac Asimov or Robert Heinlein.[190]

On the whole, though, Philip K. Dick has done very well with adaptions of his work (especially if you consider what those films *could* have turned out like, and compared to other sci-fi authors who have been treated less than successfully, to put it politely). It's a pity that Dick didn't get to see *Total Recall, Minority Report* or *A Scanner Darkly*, or the completed *Blade Runner*, but one can imagine him enjoying them.

---

[190] The one sci-fi author I'm eager to see adapted on the big screen in a full-on, mega-budget manner is Ursula Le Guin, for my money the greatest living sci-fi and fantasy author. There's been the wonderful *Tales of Earthsea*, by Studio Ghibli, of course, and the woeful *Earthsea* TV series, but when are we going to see a topnotch adaption of *The Left Hand of Darkness* or *The Dispossessed*?

FILMOGRAPHIES

BLADE RUNNER

Credits for the 1982 production

CAST

Harrison Ford – Rick Deckard
Rutger Hauer – Roy Batty
Sean Young – Rachel
Edward James Olmos – Gaff
M. Emmet Walsh – Bryant
Daryl Hannah – Pris
William Sanderson – J.F. Sebastian
Brion James – Leon Kowalski
Joe Turkel – Dr. Eldon Tyrell
Joanna Cassidy – Zhora
James Hong – Hannibal Chew
Morgan Paull – Holden
Kevin Thompson – Bear
John Edward Allen – Kaiser
Hy Pyke – Taffey Lewis
Kimiko Hiroshige – Cambodian Lady
Bob Okazaki – Howie Lee
Carolyn DeMirjian – Saleslady
Ben Astar – Abdul Ben Hassan
Judith Burnett – Ming-Fa
Leo Gorcey Jr. – Louie - Bartender
Sharon Hesky – Bar Patron
Kelly Hine – Showgirl

Tom Hutchinson – Bartender
Charles Knapp – Bartender
Rose Mascari – Bar Patron
Jirô Okazaki – Policeman
Steve Pope – Policeman
Robert Reiter – Policeman
Alexis Rhee – Geisha #1

CREW

Directed by Ridley Scott
Written by Hampton Fancher and David Peoples
Michael Deeley – producer
Hampton Fancher – executive producer
Brian Kelly – executive producer
Ivor Powell – associate producer
Jerry Perenchio – co-executive producer
Ridley Scott – co-producer
Run Run Shaw – co-executive producer
Bud Yorkin – co-executive producer
Music by Vangelis (music arranged, performed and produced by)
Cinematography by Jordan Cronenweth
Film Editing by Marsha Nakashima
Casting by Jane Feinberg, Mike Fenton, Marci Liroff
Production Design by Lawrence G. Paull
Art Direction by David L. Snyder
Set Decoration by Linda DeScenna, Leslie Frankenheimer, Thomas L. Roysden , Peg Cummings
Costume Design by Michael Kaplan and Charles Knode
Shirley Padgett – hair stylist
Marvin G. Westmore – makeup artist
John Chambers – prosthetic

makeups

Ana Maria Quintana – script supervisor

Alan Collis – production manager

C.O. Erickson – executive in charge of production

John W. Rogers – unit production manager

Newt Arnold – first assistant director

Morris Chapnick – second assistant director

Peter Cornberg – first assistant director

Donald Hauer – second assistant director

Victoria E. Rhodes – DGA trainee

Richard Peter Schroer – second assistant director

Stephen Dane – assistant art director

Mentor Huebner – production illustrator

Tom Southwell – production illustrator

James T. Woods – painting coordinator

John Alvin – poster artist

William Apperson – construction foreman and model maker

Charles Breen – set designer

Marco A. Campos – propmaker

Robert Clark – sculptor

Carmine Goglia – stand-by painter

Peter J. Hampton – production designer: additional scenes

Sherman Labby – production illustrator

Steven Ladish – props

Edward T. McAvoy – scenic artist

Curtis A. Schnell – set designer

Kevin Shanks – drapery man/ floor covering

William Ladd Skinner – set designer

Drew Struzan – poster artist

Michael Taylor – leadman

Gary Zink – carpenter

Gary Zink – propmaker

Terry E. Lewis – property master

Basil Lombardo – standby painter

Syd Mead – visual futurist

James F. Orendorff – construction coordinator

David Q. Quick – assistant property master

John A. Scott III – assistant property master

Arthur Shippee – assistant

property master

Bud Alper – sound mixer

Gene Ashbrook – boom operator

Graham V. Hartstone – chief dubbing mixer

Mike Hopkins – dialogue editor

Gerry Humphreys – chief dubbing mixer

Peter Pennell – sound editor

Joel Fein – sound recording mixer

John Hayward – sound re-recording mixer

Nicolas Le Messurier – sound re-recording mixer

Gordon K. McCallum – sound mixer

Brydon Baker III – cable person

Peter Baldock – assistant dialogue editor

Joe Gallagher – assistant sound editor

Greg Curtis – special effects technician

Logan Frazee – special effects technician

Terry D. Frazee – special floor effects supervisor

Steve Galich – special effects technician

Robert Cole – special effects action property foreman

Robert DeVine – special effects

Ken Estes – special effects foreman

Scott Forbes – special effects technician

Michael Backauskas – assistant effects editor: EEG

Tom Cranham – effects illustrator: EEG

Jonathan Seay – visual effects camera

Scott Squires – visual displays: DQI

George Trimmer – model maker

Hoyt Yeatman – visual displays: DQI

Gene Young – model construction

David Dryer – special photographic effects supervisor

Bud Elam – special engineering consultant: EEG

Michael L. Fink – action prop supervisor

Linda Fleisher – action prop consultant

Joyce Goldberg – production office manager: EEG

Robert D. Bailey – matte photography: EEG

David Grafton – special engineering consultant: EEG

Robert Hall – optical photography supervisor: EEG

David R. Hardberger – camera operator: EEG

Alan Harding – special camera technician: EEG

Jack Hinkle – film coordinator: EEG

Richard E. Hollander – computer engineering: EEG

Ronald Longo – camera operator: EEG

Don Baker – camera operator: EEG

Tim McHugh – camera operator: EEG

Gregory L. McMurry – electronic engineering: EEG

Virgil Mirano – still lab: EEG

George Polkinghorne – cinetechnician: EEG

Gary Randall – gaffer: EEG

Philip Barberio – optical line-up: EEG

Richard Rippel – optical line-up: EEG

Robert Spurlock – miniature technician: EEG

Mark Stetson – chief model maker: EEG

David K. Stewart – director of photography: EEG

Tama Takahashi – matte photography: EEG

Douglas Trumbull – special photographic effects supervisor

Patrick Van Auken – key grip: EEG

John C. Wash – animation and graphics: EEG

Evans Wetmore – electronic and mechanical design: EEG

Matthew Yuricich – matte artist: EEG

Richard Yuricich – special photographic effects supervisor

Thomas Baker – motion control camera

Craig Chandler – optical effects

Leslie Ekker – model maker

Bill George – miniature design and construction

Rocco Gioffre – matte artist

Bill Kent – camera operator: special photographic effects

Charles Cowles – camera operator: EEG

Michael McMillen – model maker

Michele Moen – matte artist: EEG

Tom Pahk – model maker

Christopher S. Ross – miniature design and construction

Gary Combs – stunt coordinator

Ray Bickel – stunts

Jeannie Epper – stunts

James M. Halty – stunts

Jeff Imada – stunts

Gary McLarty – stunts

Karen McLarty – stunts

Beth Nufer – stunts

Roy K. Ogata – stunts

Bobby Porter – stunts

Lee Pulford – stunt double: Joanna Cassidy

Ruth A. Redfern – stunts

Janet Brady – stunts

George Sawaya – stunts

Charles A. Tamburro – stunts

Jack Tyree – stunts

Mike Washlake – stunts

Michael Zurich – stunts

Diane Carter – stunts

Ann Chatterton – stunts

Gary Combs – stunt double: Harrison Ford

Gilbert B. Combs – stunts

Tony Cox – stunts

Rita Egleston – stunts

Gary Epper – stunts

Albert Bettcher – camera operator

Dick Colean – camera operator

Stephen Vaughan – still photographer

Michael B. Corbett – lighting technician

Adam Glick – set lighting technician

Dan Greer – assistant camera

Ernest Holzman – film loader

Michael E. Matteson – key grip

James Nordberg – generator operator

Jeff Paynter – second unit focus puller

Peter Santoro – second assistant camera

Bernie Schwartz – grip

Michael Genne – first assistant camera

Haskell Wexler – additional photographer

George D. Greer – second assistant camera

Cary Griffith – key grip

Richard Hart – lighting gaffer
Steven Poster – additional
photographer
Steven H. Smith – first assistant
camera
Robert C. Thomas – camera
operator
Brian Tufano – additional
photographer
Winnie D. Brown – costumer:
women
Bob E. Horn – costumer: men
James Lapidus – costumer: men
Linda Matthews – costumer:
women
Jan Ferris – designer sculptor
Jerry Herrin – costumer
supervisor: day crew
Les Healey – first assistant editor
Terry Rawlings – supervising
editor
R. William Zabala – assistant
editor
Peter Hollywood – additional
editing
Gail Laughton – composer:
additional music
Howard Brady Davidson –
transportation captain
Mario Simon – transportation
Vickie Alper – production
coordinator
Steve Warner – production
controller
Brian O. Haynes – production
assistant
Jeffrey A. Humphreys – studio
utility
Roland Kibbee – voice-over
engineer
Michael Neale – location
manager
Nancy Ramey – assistant
accountant
Jasmine Sabu – horse trainer
Charles A. Tamburro – helicopter
pilot
Katherine Haber – production
executive
David Scharf – electron
microscope photography
Linda Hess – production assistant
Saul Kahan – publicist
Michael Knutsen – craft service
Jerry Perenchio – presenter
Bud Yorkin – presenter
Run Run Shaw – presenter
William S. Burroughs – thanks:
for the use of the title "Blade
Runner"

Philip K. Dick – dedicated to the
memory of

RIDLEY SCOTT

Films directed by Ridley Scott

1977   *The Duellists*
1979   *Alien*
1982   *Blade Runner*
1985   *Legend*
1987   *Someone to Watch Over Me*
1989   *Black Rain*
1991   *Thelma & Louise*
1992   *1492: Conquest of Paradise*
1996   *White Squall*
1997   *G.I. Jane*
2000   *Gladiator*
2001   *Hannibal*
2001   *Black Hawk Down*
2003   *Matchstick Men*
2005   *Kingdom of Heaven*
2006   *A Good Year*
2007   *American Gangster*
2008   *Body of Lies*
2010   *Robin Hood*
2012   *Prometheus*

Antarctica, 1983)
The Bounty (1984)
Sauvage et Beau (1984)
Wonders of Life (1985)
Nosferatu a Venezia (1988)
Francesco (1989)
Mouseio Goulandri Fysikis Istorias (1990)
Bitter Moon (1992)
1492: Conquest of Paradise (1992)
De Nuremberg à Nuremberg (1994)
Kavafis (1996)
Mythodea - Music for the NASA Mission, 2001 Mars Odyssey (2001)
I Hope... (2001)
Alexander (2004)
Perfect Is the Enemy of Good (2005)
El Greco (2007)
The Seven Sages of Antiquity (2010)

VANGELIS

Select filmography

My Brother, the Traffic Policeman (1963)
Five Thousand Lies (1966)
Vortex (1967)
Sex-Power (1970)
Frenitis (1971)
L'apocalypse des animaux (1972)
Hello Jerusalem (1972)
Verve (1973)
Love (1974)
Do You Hear the Dogs Barking? (1975)
Le cantique des créatures: Georges Mathieu ou La fureur d'être (1974)
Le cantique des créatures: Georges Braque ou Le temps différent (1975)
Ace Up My Sleeve (1976)
La fête sauvage (1976)
Death of a Princess (1980)
Defiant Delta (1980)
Chariots of Fire (1981)
Missing (1982)
Blade Runner (1982)
Pablo Picasso Painter (1982)
Nankyoku Monogatari (a.k.a.

BIBLIOGRAPHY

N. Andrews. *True Myths: The Life and Times of Arnold Schwarzenegger*,
  Bloomsbury, London, 1995
R. Anobile, ed. *Alien*, Futura, London, 1979
L. Armitt, ed. *Where No Man Has Gone Before: Women and Science Fiction*,
  Routledge, London, 1991
—. *Theorising the Fantastic*, Arnold, London, 1996
J. Arroyo. *Action/ Spectacle Cinema*, British Film Institute, London, 2000
A. Balsamo. "Reading Cyborgs, Writing Feminism", *Communications*, 10, 3,
  1988, in J. Wolmark, 1999
—. *Technologies of the Gendered Body: Reading Cyborg Women*, Duke
  University Press, Durham, NC, 1996
M. Barr, ed. *Future Females, the Next Generation: New Voices and Velocities
  in Feminism Science Fiction Criticism*, Rowman & Littlefield, Lanham, MD,
  2000
R. Barringer: "Skinjobs, Humans and Radical Coding", *Jump Cut*, 41, 1997
J. Baudrillard. *America*, tr. C. Turner, Verso, London, 1988
—. *Simulacra and Simulation*, tr. S. Faria Glaser, University of Michigan Press,
  Ann Arbor, MI, 1994
—. "Disneyworld Company", *Liberation*, 4, Mch, 1996
—. *Selected Writings*, ed. M. Poster, Polity Press, Cambridge, 1998
J. Baxter. *Steven Spielberg: The Unauthorized Biography*, HarperCollins,
  London, 1996
D. Bell & B. Kennedy, eds. *The Cybercultures Reader*, Routledge, London,
  2000
M. Benedikt, ed. *Cyberspace: First Steps*, MIT Press, Cambridge, MA, 1991
C. Berg: "Immigrants, Aliens and Extraterrestrials", *Cine-Action!*, 18, 1989
P. Bizony. *2001: Filming the Future*, Aurum Press, London, 1994
D. Bordwell & K. Thompson. *Film Art: An Introduction*, McGraw-Hill
  Publishing Company, N.Y., 1979
—. *et al. The Classical Hollywood Cinema: Film Style and Mode of Product-
  ion to 1960*, Routledge, London, 1985
—. *Narration in the Fiction Film*, Routledge, London, 1988
—. *The Way Hollywood Tells It*, University of California Press, CA, 2006
F. Botting. *Making Monstrous: Frankenstein, Criticism, Theory*, Manchester
  University Press, Manchester, 1991
—. *Gothic*, Routledge, London, 1996
—. *Sex, Machines and Novels: Fiction, Fantasy and History in the Future
  Present*, Manchester University Press, Manchester, 1999
S. Brewster *et al*, eds. *Inhuman Reflections: Thinking the Limits of the
  Human*, Manchester University Press, Manchester, 2000
P. Brooker, ed. *Modernism/ Postmodernism*, Longman, London, 1992
A. Brooks. *Postfeminisms: Feminism, Cultural Theory and Cultural Forms*,
  Routledge, London, 1997
J. Brosnan. *Future Tense: The Cinema of Science Fiction*, St Martin's, New
  York, N.Y., 1978
—. *Primal Screen: A History of Science Fiction Film*, Orbit, London, 1991
S. Bukatman. "Postcards From the Posthuman Solar System", *Science Fiction*

Studies, 55, 1991

—. Terminal Identity: The Virtual Subject in Postmodern Science Fiction, Duke University Press, Durham, NC, 1993

—. "The Artificial Infinite", in L. Cooke, 1995

—. Blade Runner, British Film Institute, London, 1997

—. "The Ultimate Trip: Special Effects and Kaleidoscopic Perception", Iris, 25, 1998

L. Cherny & E.R. Weise, eds. Wired Women: Gender and New Realities in Cyberspace, Seal Press, Seattle, WA, 1996

S. Cohan & I.R. Hark, eds. Screening the Male: Exploring Masculinities in Hollywood Cinema, Routledge, London, 1993

L. Cooke & P. Wollen, eds. Visual Display, Bay Press, Seattle, WA, 1995

B. Creed. "Alien and the Monstrous-Feminine", in A. Kuhn, 1990

—. The Monstrous-Feminine, Routledge, London, 1993

M. Deeley. Blade Runners, Deer Hunters and Blowing the Bloody Doors Off, Faber, London, 2008

M. Dery, ed. Flame Wars: The Discourse of Cyberculture, Duke University Press, Durham, NC, 1994

—. Escape Velocity: Cyberculture At the End of the Century, Hodder, 1996

P. Dick. Minority Report, Gollancz, London, 2002

J. Dixon & E. Cassidy, eds. Virtual Futures: Cyberotics, Technology and Post-human Pragmatism, Routledge, London, 1998

M. Doel & D. Clark. From Pastiche To the Screening of the Eye? Or, Geo-graphies of a Diegesis: Postmodernism, Hyperspace and Simulation in the Screening of Blade Runner, University of Leeds Press, Leeds, 1999

M. Doane. "Technophilia", in J. Wolmark, 1999

J. Donald, ed. Fantasy and the Cinema, BFI, London, 1989

M. Featherstone & R. Burrows, eds. Cyberspace/ Cyberbodies/ Cyberpunk, Sage, London, 1995

C. Finch. Special Effects, Abbeville, New York, N.Y., 1984

I. Freer. The Complete Spielberg, Virgin Publishing, London, 2001

C. Fuchs: "Death Is Irrelevant: Cyborgs, Reproduction, and the Future of Male Hysteria", Gender, 18, 1993

J. Gallagher. Film Directors On Directing, Praeger, New York, NY, 1989

K. Gelder, ed. The Horror Reader, Routledge, London, 2000

W. Gibson. Neuromancer, Grafton, London, 1986

F. Glass: "The 'New Bad Future': Robocop and 1980s Sci-Fi Films", Science as Culture, 5, 1989

L. Goldberg et al, eds. Science Fiction Filmmaking in the 1980s, McFarland, Jefferson, 1995

J. González. "Envisioning Cyborg Bodies", in G. Gray, 1995

A. Gordon. "Science-fiction and fantasy film criticism: the case of Lucas and Spielberg", Journal of the Fantastic in the Arts, 2, 2, 1989

B.K. Grant, ed. Planks of Reason: Essays on the Horror Film, Scarecrow Press, N.J., 1984

—. ed. Crisis Cinema: The Apocalyptic Idea in Postmodern Narrative Film, Maisonneuve Press, 1993

—. Film Genre Reader II, University of Texas Press, Austin, TX, 1995

—. ed. The Dread of Difference: Gender and the Horror Film, University of Texas Press, Austin, TX, 1996

C. Gray, ed. The Cyborg Handbook, Routledge, London, 1995

E. Grosz. Volatile Bodies, Indiana University Press, Bloomington, IN, 1994

—. Space, Time and Perversion, Routledge, London, 1995

D. Haraway. "A Manifesto For Cyborgs", Socialist Review, 15, 2, 1985

—. Primate Visions: Gender, Race and Nature in the World of Modern Science, Routledge, London, 1989

—. Simians, Cyborgs, and Women, Routledge, London, 1991a

—. "Cyborgs At Large", Social Text, 25, 1991b

P. Hardy, ed. The Aurum Encyclopedia of Science Fiction, Aurum, London, 1991

E.R. Helford, ed. *Fantasy Girls: Gender in the New Universe of Science Fiction and Fantasy TV*, Rowman & Littlefield, Lanham, MD, 2000

J. Howard. *The Complete Films of Orson Welles*, Citadel Press, N.Y., 1991

—. *The Stanley Kubrick Companion*, Batsford, London, 1999

D. Hughes. *The Complete Kubrick*, Virgin, 2000

I.Q. Hunter. *British Science Fiction Cinema*, Routledge, London, 1999

F. Jameson. *Signatures of the Visible*, Routledge, N.Y., 1990

—. *Postmodernism, or the Cultural Logic of Late Capitalism*, Verso, London, 1991

—. & M. Miyoshi, eds. *Cultures of Globalization*, Duke University Press, Durham, NC, 1998

S. Jeffords. *Hard Bodies: Hollywood Masculinity in the Reagan Era*, Rutgers University Press, New Brunswick, NJ, 1994

G. Jenkins. *Empire Building: The Remarkable Real Life Story of Star Wars*, Simon & Schuster, N.Y., 1997

W. Johnson. *Focus on the Science Fiction Film*, Prentice-Hall, N.J., 1972

S. Jones, ed. *Virtual Culture*, Sage, London, 1997

M. Kellner *et al.* "*Blade Runner*", *Jump Cut*, 29, 1984

J. Kerman, ed. *Retrofitting Blade Runner*, Bowling Green State University Popular Press, 1991

G. King. *Spectacular Narratives: Hollywood in the Age of the Blockbuster*, I.B. Tauris, London, 2000

—. & T. Krzywinmska. *Science Fiction Cinema*, Wallflower, London, 2000

P. Kolker. *The Altering Eye: Contemporary International Cinema*, Oxford University Press, N.Y., 1983

—. *A Cinema of Loneliness: Penn, Kubrick, Coppola, Scorsese, Altman*, Oxford University Press, N.Y., 1988

A. & M. Kroker, eds. *Body Invaders: Panic Sex in America*, St Martin's Press, N. Y., 1988

—. eds. *The Hysterical Male: New Feminist Theory*, St Martin's Press, N.Y., 1991

—. *Hacking the Future*, New World Perspectives, Montréal, 1996

—. *Digital Delirium*, New World Perspectives, Montréal, 1997

A. Kuhn, ed. *Alien Zone: Cultural Theory and Contemporary Science Fiction*, Verso, London, 1990

—. ed. *Alien Zone 2*, Verso, London, 1999

A. Landsberg: "Prosthetic Memory: *Total Recall* and *Blade Runner*", in M. Featherstone, 1995

S. Lefanu. *In the Chinks of the World Machine: Feminism and Science Fiction*, Women's Press, London, 1988

H. Lightman. "*Blade Runner*", *American Cinematographer*, 1982

J. McBride. *Steven Spielberg*, Faber, London, 1997

D. Menville & R. Reginald. *Future Visions: The New Golden Age of the Science Fiction Film*, Newcastle, CA, 1985

J. Murray. *Hamlet On the Holodeck: The Future of Narrative in Cyberspace*, MIT Press, Cambridge, MA, 1997

D. Neumann, ed. *Film Architecture: From Metropolis to Blade Runner*, Prestel-Verlag, New York, NY, 1996

C. Penley, ed. *Feminism and Film Theory*, Routledge, London, 1988

—. "Time Travel, Prime Scene and the Critical Dystopia", *Camera Obscura*, 15, 1988

—. *et al*, eds. *Close Encounters: Film, Feminism and Science Fiction*, University of Minnesota Press, Minneapolis, 1991

—. & A. Ross, eds. *Technoculture*, University of Minnesota Press, Minneapolis, 1991

M. Pierson. "CGI effects in Hollywood science fiction cinema", *Screen*, 40, 2, Summer, 1999

C. Platt, ed. *Dream Makers: Science Fiction and Fantasy Writers At Work*, Xanadu, London, 1986

D. Pollock. *Skywalking: The Life and Films of George Lucas*, Crown, N.Y.,

1983, 1990, 2000

E. Rabkin & G. Slusser, eds. *Shadows of the Magic Lamp: Fantasy and Science Fiction in Film*, Southern Illinois University Press, Carbondale, 1985

—. *Aliens: The Anthropology of Science Fiction*, Southern Illinois University Press, Carbondale, IL, 1987

N. Ruddick, ed. *State of the Fantastic*, Greenwood Press, New York, N.Y., 1992

J. Rusher & T. Frentz. *Projecting the Shadow: The Cyborg Hero in American Film*, University of Chicago Press, IL, 1995

B. Rux. *Hollywood vs. the Aliens*, Frog, Berkeley, 1997

P. Sammon. "Do Androids Dream of Unicorns? The 7 Faces of *Blade Runner*", *Video Watchdog*, 20, Dec, 1993

—. *Future Noir: The Making of Blade Runner*, Orion Media, London, 1996

—. "Bug Bytes: *Starship Troopers*", *Cinefex*, 73, Mch, 1998

—. *The Making of Starship Troopers*, Little, Brown, Boston, MA, 1999

—. *Ridley Scott*, Orion, London, 1999

D. Schaefer & L. Salvato, eds. *Masters of Light*, University of California Press, Berkeley, CA, 1984

P. Schelde. *Androids, Humanoids and Other Science Fiction Monsters*, New York University Press, N.Y., 1993

G. Schwab: "Cyborgs", *Discourse*, 9, 1987

T. Shone. *Blockbuster: How the Jaws and Jedi Generation Turned Hollywood Into a Boom-Town*, Scribner, London, 2005

K. Silverman. *The Acoustic Mirror: The Female Voice in Psychoanalysis and Cinema*, Indiana University Press, Bloomington, IN, 1988

—. "Back to the Future", *Camera Obscura*, 27, 1991

V. Sobchack. *The Limits of Infinity: The American Science Fiction Film*, A.S. Barnes, N.Y., 1980

—. *Screening Space: The American Science Fiction Film*, Ungar, N.Y., 1987/ 1993

—. "Cities On the Edge of Time: The Urban Science Fiction Film", *East-West Film Journal*, 3, 1, Dec, 1988

—. *The Address of the Eye: A Phenomenology of Film Experience*, Princeton University Press, N.J., 1992

—. ed. *The Persistence of History: Cinema, Television, and the Modern Event*, Routledge, London, 1995

C. Springer. "The Pleasure of the Interface", *Screen*, 32, 3, 1991

—. "Muscular Circuitry", *Genders*, 18, 1993

—. *Electronic Eros*, Athlone, London, 1996

G. Stewart. *Between Film and Screen: Modernism's Photo Synthesis*, University of Chicago Press, Chicago, IL, 1999

Y. Tasker. *Spectacular Bodies: Gender, Genre and the Action Cinema*, Routledge, London, 1993

D. Thomson. *The Alien Quartet*, Bloomsbury, London, 1998

K. Van Gunden. *Fantasy Films*, McFarland, Jefferson, N.C. 1989

—. *Postmodern Auteurs: Coppola, Lucas, De Palma, Spielberg and Scorsese*, McFarland, Jefferson, N.C. 1991

R. van Scheers. *Paul Verhoeven*, Faber, London, 1997

M.C. Vaz. *From Star Wars to Indiana Jones*, Chronicle, San Francisco, CA, 1994

—. & P.R. Duignan. *Industrial Light & Magic*, Virgin, London, 1996

P. Verhoeven. *Paul Verhoeven: Beyond Flesh and Blood*, Le Cinépage, Cinéditions, Paris, 2001

P. Virilio & S. Lotringer. *War and Cinema*, Verso, London, 1992

—. *The Vision Machine*, tr. J. Rose, Indiana University Press, Bloomington, IN, 1994

Walsh. *"Minority Report" Official Strategy Guide*, Brady Games, 2002

P. Warrick: *The Cybernetic Imagination in Science Fiction*, MIT Press, 1980

O. Welles. *Orson Welles: Interviews*, ed. M. Estrin, University of Mississippi

Press, Jackson, 2002

D. Wingrove, ed. *Science Fiction Film Source Book*, Longman, London, 1985

J. Wolmark. *Aliens and Others: Science Fiction, Feminism and Postmodernism*, Harvester Wheatsheaf, 1993

—. ed. *Cybersexualities: A Reader on Feminist Theory, Cyborgs and Cyberspace*, Edinburgh University Press, Edinburgh, 1999

S. Zizek. *Enjoy Your Symptom Jacques Lacan in Hollywood and Out*, Routledge, New York, NY, 1992

—. *Tarrying With the Negative: Kant, Hegel, and the Critique of Ideology*, Duke University Press, Durham, NC, 1993

ARTS, PAINTING, SCULPTURE

web: www.crmoon.com • e-mail: cresmopub@yahoo.co.uk

The Art of Andy Goldsworthy
Andy Goldsworthy: Touching Nature
Andy Goldsworthy in Close-Up
Andy Goldsworthy: Pocket Guide
Andy Goldsworthy In America
Land Art: A Complete Guide
The Art of Richard Long
Richard Long: Pocket Guide
Land Art In Great Britain
Land Art in Close-Up
Land Art In the U.S.A.
Land Art: Pocket Guide
Installation Art in Close-Up
Minimal Art and Artists In the 1960s and After
Colourfield Painting
Land Art DVD, TV documentary
Andy Goldsworthy DVD, TV documentary
The Erotic Object: Sexuality in Sculpture From Prehistory to the Present Day
Sex in Art: Pornography and Pleasure in Painting and Sculpture
Postwar Art
Sacred Gardens: The Garden in Myth, Religion and Art
Glorification: Religious Abstraction in Renaissance and 20th Century Art
Early Netherlandish Painting
Jasper Johns
Brice MardenLeonardo da Vinci
Piero della Francesca
Giovanni Bellini
Fra Angelico: Art and Religion in the Renaissance
Mark Rothko: The Art of Transcendence
Frank Stella: American Abstract Artist
Alison Wilding: The Embrace of Sculpture
Vincent van Gogh: Visionary Landscapes
Eric Gill: Nuptials of God
Constantin Brancusi: Sculpting the Essence of Things
Max Beckmann
Gustave Moreau
Caravaggio
Egon Schiele: Sex and Death In Purple Stockings
Delizioso Fotografico Fervore: Works In Process 1
Sacro Cuore: Works In Process 2
The Light Eternal: J.M.W. Turner
The Madonna Glorified: Karen Arthurs

LITERATURE

J.R.R. Tolkien: The Books, The Films, The Whole Cultural Phenomenon
J.R.R. Tolkien: Pocket Guide
Beauties, Beasts and Enchantment: Classic French Fairy Tales
Tolkien's Heroic Quest
Brothers Grimm: German Popular Stories
Sexing Hardy: Thomas Hardy and Feminism
Thomas Hardy's *Tess of the d'Urbervilles*
Thomas Hardy's *Jude the Obscure*
Thomas Hardy: The Tragic Novels
Love and Tragedy: Thomas Hardy
The Poetry of Landscape in Hardy
Wessex Revisited: Thomas Hardy and John Cowper Powys
Wolfgang Iser: Essays and Interviews
Petrarch, Dante and the Troubadours
Maurice Sendak and the Art of Children's Book Illustration
Andrea Dworkin
Cixous, Irigaray, Kristeva: The *Jouissance* of French Feminism
Julia Kristeva: Art, Love, Melancholy, Philosophy, Semiotics and Psychoanalysis
Hélene Cixous I Love You: The *Jouissance* of Writing
Luce Irigaray: Lips, Kissing, and the Politics of Sexual Difference
Peter Redgrove: Here Comes the Flood
Peter Redgrove: Sex-Magic-Poetry-Cornwall
Lawrence Durrell: Between Love and Death, East and West
Love, Culture & Poetry: Lawrence Durrell
Cavafy: Anatomy of a Soul
German Romantic Poetry: Goethe, Novalis, Heine, Hölderlin
Novalis: *Hymns To the Night*
Feminism and Shakespeare
Shakespeare: *The Sonnets*
Shakespeare: Love, Poetry & Magic
The Passion of D.H. Lawrence
D.H. Lawrence: Symbolic Landscapes
D.H. Lawrence: Infinite Sensual Violence
The Ecstasies of John Cowper Powys
Sensualism and Mythology: The Wessex Novels of John Cowper Powys
Amorous Life: John Cowper Powys (H.W. Fawkner)
Postmodern Powys: New Essays on John Cowper Powys (Joe Boulter)
Rethinking Powys: Critical Essays on John Cowper Powys
Paul Bowles & Bernardo Bertolucci
Rainer Maria Rilke
Joseph Conrad: *Heart of Darkness*
In the Dim Void: Samuel Beckett
Samuel Beckett Goes into the Silence
André Gide: Fiction and Fervour
Jackie Collins and the Blockbuster Novel
Blinded By Her Light: The Love-Poetry of Robert Graves

POETRY

Ursula Le Guin: *Walking In Cornwall*
Peter Redgrove: Here Comes The Flood
Peter Redgrove: Sex-Magic-Poetry-Cornwall
Dante: Selections From the *Vita Nuova*
Petrarch, Dante and the Troubadours
William Shakespeare: *The Sonnets*
William Shakespeare: Complete Poems
Blinded By Her Light: The Love-Poetry of Robert Graves
Emily Dickinson: Selected Poems
Emily Brontë: Poems
Thomas Hardy: Selected Poems
Percy Bysshe Shelley: Poems
John Keats: Selected Poems
John Keats: Poems of 1820
D.H. Lawrence: Selected Poems
Edmund Spenser: Poems
Edmund Spenser: *Amoretti*
John Donne: Poems
Henry Vaughan: Poems
Sir Thomas Wyatt: Poems
Robert Herrick: Selected Poems
Rilke: Space, Essence and Angels in the Poetry of Rainer Maria Rilke
Rainer Maria Rilke: Selected Poems
Friedrich Hölderlin: Selected Poems
Arseny Tarkovsky: Selected Poems
Paul Verlaine: Selected Poems
Novalis: *Hymns To the Night*
Arthur Rimbaud: Selected Poems
Arthur Rimbaud: *A Season in Hell*
Arthur Rimbaud and the Magic of Poetry
D.J. Enright: By-Blows
Jeremy Reed: *Brigitte's Blue Heart*
Jeremy Reed: *Claudia Schiffer's Red Shoes*
Gorgeous Little Orpheus
Radiance: New Poems
Crescent Moon Book of Nature Poetry
Crescent Moon Book of Love Poetry
Crescent Moon Book of Mystical Poetry
Crescent Moon Book of Elizabethan Love Poetry
Crescent Moon Book of Metaphysical Poetry
Crescent Moon Book of Romantic Poetry
Pagan America: New American Poetry

MEDIA, CINEMA, FEMINISM and CULTURAL STUDIES

J.R.R. Tolkien: The Books, The Films, The Whole Cultural Phenomenon
J.R.R. Tolkien: Pocket Guide
The *Lord of the Rings* Movies: Pocket Guide
The Ghost Dance: The Origins of Religion
The Cinema of Hayao Miyazaki
Hayao Miyazaki: *Princess Mononoke*: Pocket Movie Guide
Hayao Miyazaki: *Spirited Away*: Pocket Movie Guide
The Peyote Cult
HomeGround: The Kate Bush Anthology
Tim Burton : Hallowe'en For Hollywood
Ken Russell
Cixous, Irigaray, Kristeva: The *Jouissance* of French Feminism
Julia Kristeva: Art, Love, Melancholy, Philosophy, Semiotics and Psychoanalysis
Luce Irigaray: Lips, Kissing, and the Politics of Sexual Difference
Hélène Cixous I Love You: The *Jouissance* of Writing
Andrea Dworkin
'Cosmo Woman': The World of Women's Magazines
Women in Pop Music
Discovering the Goddess (Geoffrey Ashe)
The Poetry of Cinema
The Sacred Cinema of Andrei Tarkovsky
Andrei Tarkovsky: Pocket Guide
Andrei Tarkovsky: *Mirror*: Pocket Movie Guide
Walerian Borowczyk: Cinema of Erotic Dreams
Jean-Luc Godard: The Passion of Cinema
Jean-Luc Godard: Pocket Guide
John Hughes and Eighties Cinema
Ferris Buller's Day Off: Pocket Movie Guide
The Cinema of Richard Linklater
Liv Tyler: Star In Ascendance
Blade Runner and the Films of Philip K. Dick
Paul Bowles and Bernardo Bertolucci
Media Hell: Radio, TV and the Press
Detonation Britain: Nuclear War in the UK
Feminism and Shakespeare
Wild Zones: Pornography, Art and Feminism
Sex in Art: Pornography and Pleasure in Painting and Sculpture
Sexing Hardy: Thomas Hardy and Feminism

The Light Eternal is a model monograph, an exemplary job. The subject matter of the book is beautifully organised and dead on beam. (Lawrence Durrell)
It is amazing for me to see my work treated with such passion and respect. (Andrea Dworkin)
Sex-Magic-Poetry-Cornwall is a very rich essay... It is like a brightly-lighted box. (Peter Redgrove)

CRESCENT MOON PUBLISHING P.O. Box 1312, Maidstone, Kent, ME14 5XU, Great Britain
0044-1622-729593 cresmopub@yahoo.co.uk www.crmoon.com

www.ingramcontent.com/pod-product-compliance
Lightning Source LLC
Chambersburg PA
CBHW062109080426
42734CB00012B/2810